The Letters of Alcuin

Rolph Barlow Page

Alpha Editions

This edition published in 2020

ISBN : 9789354034831

Design and Setting By
Alpha Editions
email - alphaedis@gmail.com

TO MY WIFE

PREFACE

THE life of Alcuin has been written many times; and the Carolingian Age in which he played no mean part has often been fully treated. The present work is concerned with neither of these, primarily, yet both will necessarily be discussed in some measure in connection with its main purpose, which is to determine how far Alcuin's life and works mirror forth his age, and to what extent they influenced the events of that time.

The author wishes to thank his colleagues in the New York High School of Commerce, Messrs. Carleton, Lewis and Wharton, for the valuable assistance they have given him in the final preparation of the manuscript. To Professor James T. Shotwell, at whose instance the author entered Columbia University, he is especially indebted for many kindnesses and for many helpful suggestions in the writing and revising of this work. His sincerest thanks are due to Professor James Harvey Robinson, at whose suggestion this work was undertaken, and without whose encouragement it would never have been completed.

R. B. P.

NEW YORK CITY, April, 1909.

CONTENTS

INTRODUCTION

The value of Alcuin's letters as sources for the age of Charles the Great—Alcuin's early life and career in England; his birth and education at York—His teaching at York—His pilgrimage to Rome—Meeting with Charles the Great and invitation to Frankland—Master of the Palace School—Alcuin returns to England to make peace between Charles the Great and Offa, king of Mercia—His return to Frankland; opposition to Adoptionism and Image-Worship—Abbot of Tours; his quarrel with Theodulph of Orleans and King Charles—His restoration to favor and peaceful death.

CHAPTER I

ALCUIN'S THEOLOGICAL RÔLE

The general nature of Alcuin's theology; his attitude towards the Church Fathers—His struggle against the Adoptionists; dogmatic works against the latter; nature and origin of Adoptionism; course of the struggle; its significance. Other dogmatic works—Part played by Alcuin in the controversies over *filioque* and Image-Worship—Exegetical works of Alcuin; their nature and purpose—The Commentaries; his method of interpretation; influence and importance of his exegetical works—Moral and biographical works; their lack of originality—Conclusion.

CHAPTER II

SOCIAL AND POLITICAL CONDITIONS

THE Papacy as portrayed by Alcuin; its difficulties, its weakness—Relations with the Frankish power—The Frankish Church and Charles the Great; his ecclesiastical policy and reforms; Alcuin's influence upon these—The Empire; Alcuin's conception of it—Social conditions in Frankland in Alcuin's day—The clergy, princes and common people—Social conditions in England; internal strife; devastations by the Northmen—Remedial measures—Conclusion.

CHAPTER III

ALCUIN AS A TEACHER

GENERAL condition of learning in the seventh and eighth centuries—The educational aims of Alcuin and Charles—Lack of schools, teachers and books; a mediæval library—The schools of Charles the Great—Alcuin and the Palace School—The subjects taught; the Seven Liberal Arts; Alcuin's educational works—Alcuin's attitude toward the classics; his literary style, methods and discipline—Results and conclusions.

INTRODUCTION

In the following pages an attempt will be made to form an estimate of some of the more important phases of the work of Alcuin, from the traces which have come down to us in his own works and in those of the men with whom he came most in contact. The principal source used is his correspondence supplemented by his other works, dogmatic, exegetical, moral and didactic. Where these have proved inadequate, further evidence has been sought in the Carolingian Capitularies and other contemporary sources. The correspondence of Alcuin, as preserved, includes not merely his own letters, but the replies of others, and so especially commends itself by reason of its scope and nature. In all, there are in the collection three hundred and eleven letters,[1]

(1) For the earlier editions of Alcuin's correspondence see Potthast, *Wegweiser*, p. 34. A modern and very excellent edition is the one prepared by Jaffé, and published by Wattenbach and Duemmler in 1873 in the sixth volume of the *Bibliotheca Rerum Germanicarum*. This has a decided advantage over the preceding editions in that it has incorporated with the 306 letters which it contains the three most valuable sources for the life of Alcuin. These are, the *Vita Alchuini Auctore anonymo*, probably written by Sigulfus (cf. Jaffé *op. cit.* p. 1), and the *Vita Sancti Willibrordi*, and *Versus de Sanctis Eboracensis Ecclesiæ*, written by Alcuin himself. However, in view of the investigations of Sickel, and of Duemmler himself, the edition was soon in need of revision so far as the arrangement of the letters was concerned. Moreover, though the editors had heartily approved of the major part of the work prepared by their dead friend Jaffé, it had not been entirely satisfactory to them. Accordingly, Duemmler prepared a new edition which was published in 1895 in the *Monumenta Germaniæ Historica, Epistolarum*, Volume IV, pps. 1-493. It is based very largely on that of Jaffé, but it rejects one or two untrustworthy sources used by the latter. Duemmler has also revised the dates of many of the letters and has rearranged the whole correspondence. Moreover, while omitting six of the letters inserted in the edition of Jaffé he has made considerable additions to four others, (Epp. 3, 28, 49, 145) and has incorporated in his own edition eleven letters which were not known to Jaffé or rejected by him. It is to this edition that references will

penned by the choicest spirits of the age, among them such
men as Angilbert, Adalhard, Leidrad, Theodulph, Benedict of Aniane, Paulinus, Arno and Charles the Great himself. As an intimate friend and zealous co-laborer with
these in an endeavor to elevate the whole Frankish people
to the level of that civilization which still lingered on in
some of the more fortunate places of the realm, Alcuin's
correspondence with each and all of them is well-nigh indispensable to those who would obtain a proper conception of the political and social history of his day. Therein
the whole inner life of the Carolingian Age is reflected for
our inspection. The Frankish nobility, as Alcuin knew it
at the court and in the Palace School, vigorous, but untutored; the Frankish clergy, unorganized, vitiated by
ignorance and sloth, impelled to reform by the genius of its
king; the struggling Papacy, beset by foes within and without; barbarian peoples accepting Christianity and civilization at the point of the sword; a great Christian empire
in the making—all these stand out in the correspondence
of Alcuin in a way that is most illuminating. Moreover,
an especial significance and value attaches to Alcuin's
letters, by reason of the fact that he regards himself as a
mentor and father-confessor to the foremost people of his
time. He assumed to write with the confidence of a pope
to every region, parish, province and state of his world,
exhorting and admonishing the people after the fashion of
the holy fathers.[1] As a matter of fact, there is scarcely a

---

be made in these pages. See also, Sickel, Th., *Alcuinstudien* in
Sitzungsberichte der Philosophisch-Historischen Classe der Wiener
Akademie, Vol. LXXIX. Sybel's *Historische Zeitschrift*, Vol. XXXII,
pp. 352-365. Duemmler E., *Zur Lebensgeschichte Alcuins* in Neues
Archiv, Vol. XVIII, pp. 51-70. Duemmler, E., *Introduction to Alcuin's
Letters*, M. G. H., Epistolarum, Vol. IV, pp. 1 et seq.

(1) "Et litteris sub eius (papae) sancti nominis auctoritate per
diversas mundi regiones populos parrochias civitates et provincias
hortari; et catholicae fidei rationes plurioribus exponere personis."
Ep 179.

question of the day of any importance in church or state
on which Alcuin does not express an opinion. It is his
sense of varied personal responsibility which makes
his letters so rich in material, and therefore so valuable a supplement to the other scanty sources for this time.

The data for the life of Alcuin are very scanty. The
exact time of his birth cannot be fixed; but it would appear
that he was born in Northumbria between the years 730 and
735 A. D.[1] According to the statement of his biographer,
he was of noble birth,[2] and he himself claimed that he was
related to St. Willibrord's father, a nobleman of Northumbria.[3] His early life, according to his own testimony, was
spent in the monastery at York, where he was most kindly
treated by his masters, Egbert and Aelbert.[4] Here, in com-
pany with other youths of noble birth, he was instructed
by the good Aelbert in all the learning of the Seven Liberal
Arts.[5] He evinced the liveliest interest in his studies,
especially in Virgil, and soon became the best pupil in the
school. As such he was the recipient of an unusually
large share of that affection which his master Aelbert was
wont to lavish on all his pupils.

Consequently, when Aelbert made a pilgrimage to Rome,
after the fashion of scholars of the time, to find something
new in the way of books and studies,[6] he was accompanied

(1) Frobenius, Mabillon and Lorentz, whom most of the later
biographers follow, state that Alcuin's birth could not have occurred
earlier than 735; Duemmler, on the other hand, argues that Alcuin was
probably born about 730. Cf. Lorentz *Alkuin*, p. 9: Duemmler, E., *Zur
Lebensgeschichte Alchuins* in Gesellschaft für ältere Deutsche Geschichtskunde, Neues Archiv, Vol. XVIII, 1893, p. 54
(2) *Vita Alchuini Auctore anonymo*, chap. 1, apud Jaffé, Biblotheca
Rerum Germanicarum, Vol. VI, p. 6.
(3) *Vita Sancti Willibrordi*, chap. 1. Jaffé, *op. cit.*, pp. 40, 41, 76.
Epp. 20, 19, 43, 47.
(4) *Ep.* 42. *Versus de SS. Ebor. Eccles. op. cit.*, vv. 1648-1652. Cf.
Epp. 114, 121, 116, 143, 148.
(5) *Versus de SS. Ebor. Eccles. op. cit.*, vv. 1430-1452, 1515, 1522,
1530.
(6) "Hic quoque Romuleam venit devotus ad urbem." *Versus de
SS. Ebor. Eccles. op. cit.*, vv. 1457, 1458. Cf. "Quos (libellos) habui

by his favorite pupil, Alcuin. The two Anglo-Saxon
monks, master and pupil, passed through Frankland, and
such was the impression made upon the latter that he desired to remain with the Alsatian monks of Murbach.[1]
Though Alcuin dismisses the subject of his sojourn in
Rome with a short but reverential mention,[2] there is little
room to doubt that the ancient home of the Cæsars made
a great impression upon him. Their journey had some
noteworthy incidents; at Pavia, they heard Peter of Pisa
hold a disputation with a certain Lullus, and later on they
met King Charles himself.[3]

On their return to York, Alcuin continued to aid Aelbert
in the work of the school. Soon a change came; Aelbert
succeeded to the archbishopric on the death of Egbert in
766, while Alcuin became master of the school, and was
given express care of the books, those invaluable treasures
which he and his master had been at such infinite pains to
collect.[4] Alcuin's reputation as a teacher and scholar
attracted many pupils to his school at York. Among these
were some from abroad, and others whom he frequently
mentions in his letters.[5] He taught them what he himself
had studied, namely, the Seven Liberal Arts.[6] Like
Aelbert, he was a successful teacher; his pupils ever remembered him with gratitude and affection. Indeed, at this
stage of his career, his lines were cast in pleasant places,
and later he speaks of this period of his life with regret.

in patria per bonam et devotissimam magistri mei industriam vel etiam
mei ipsius qualemcumque sudorem," *Ep.* 121. Cf. Alcuin's Epitaph on
Aelbert, M. G. H. Poet. Lat. Med. Aev. I p. 206.

(1) *Epp* 172, 271. (2) *Versus de SS. Ebor. Eccles. op. cit.*, vv.
1457, 1458. (3) *Ep.* 172.

(4) *Vita Alchuini, op. cit.,* chap. 5. Cf. *Ep.* 121.

(5) Among these were Eanbald, the Second, Archbishop of York,
and Sigulfus, who followed him to France. Chief among those from
abroad were Liudger, and Albert, sent from Gregory of Frisia. *Vita
Alchuini op. cit.,* chap. 11. Cf. *Vita S. Liudgeri,* M. G. H. SS. II, p.
407. Cf. *Epp.* 112, 290.

(6) *Versus de SS. Ebor. Eccles. op. cit.,* vv. 1535-1561.

When not engaged in teaching, he spent his leisure time
with his old master, Aelbert, whom he honored as a scholar
and loved as a father.[1] When Aelbert died in 788 A. D., *778*
Alcuin mourned him with the most touching sorrow, and
it may be, as one of his biographers suggests, that the death
of his old master was one of the factors which determined
him to go to Frankland.

In 781 he went to Rome to obtain the pallium for Eanbald.[2] During the journey he met Charles at Parma, was
invited to make his home in Frankland, and, after hesitat-
ing until he should obtain the consent of his archbishop
and of his king, he betook himself with their permission
to the palace of Charles at Aachen in 782. Here he received
a warm welcome from the king,[3] and was shortly after
given charge of certain abbeys.[4]

The motive which induced Alcuin to leave England was
probably not so much the death of his beloved master as
his recognition of the fact that conditions there were
far from conducive to the advancement of learning.[5]
And then it must be remembered that Frankland had a
great fascination for our English scholar. He was an enthusiastic admirer of Charles, whom he regarded not only
as the defender of the Church, but as a mighty conqueror
extending his conquests to enlarge the domain of civilization. Again, Frankland offered a splendid opportunity for
work as well as for glory. The monasteries had been destroyed or their property devastated; learning had decreased

(1) *Ep* 148, p. 239. Cf. *Versus de SS. Ebor. Eccles. op. cit.,* vv.
1589-1595.
(2) *Vita Alchuini op. cit.,* chap. 5, p. 17. Cf. authorities quoted in
Jaffé VI. *op. cit.,* p. 17, note 1.
(3) *Vita Alchuini op. cit.,* chap. 5, p. 17. Cf. Einhard, *Vita Caroli
imperatoris,* chap. 25, M. G. H. SS. II. p. 456: Theodulph *Carmen* 25,
Ad Carolum Regem, vv. 131-140, M. G. H. Poet. Lat. Med. Aev. Vol.
I. p. 486.
(4) *Epp.* 153, 154, 232.
(5) *Epp.* 101, 102, 109, 122.

from generation to generation; the very language had been debased; the manuscripts, even those relating to the saints, had been neglected or mutilated. Alcuin, as might have been expected, seems to have regarded his mission to Frankland as an apostleship of religion, rather than of learning. "I have not come to Frankland," he says, "nor remained there for love of money, but for the sake of religion and the strengthening of the Catholic faith."[1]

Alcuin's first and most important work in Frankland was to act as Charles' chief co-laborer in the restoration of letters—a herculean task, the consummation of which the king regarded as second only to the maintenance of the kingdom itself. For this task, Alcuin was eminently fitted by his learning, his affiliations with the church,[2] and above all, by his practical turn of mind and his admiration for the genius and plans of King Charles. He began his work by teaching the Seven Liberal Arts in the Palace School. The pupils were the youths of the court, young men destined for high office in church and state. Charles, himself, and his elders were wont to participate in the discussions, when the affairs of state were not too urgent.[3]

His position as master of the Palace School was no sinecure. He had a mixed class, old and young, men and women; all of them curious, eager, insistent, plying him with questions that at times must have been most disconcerting. Not the least of his difficulties was that his pupils gloried in the martial supremacy of their race, and could

(1) *Epp.* 178, 198, 171, 41, 217, 43. Cf. Alcuin's *Adversus Elipandum*, bk. I, chap. 16, Migne CCI, p. 251.

(2) His biographer states that though he had never taken vows, yet he lived a life no less self-denying than the most strict adherent of the Benedictine Rule. Cf. *Vita Alchuini op. cit.*, chap 8. In this connection see Gaskoin's article *"Was Alcuin a Monk?"* Appendix 1 Gaskoin *"Alcuin"* pp. 249-252; Hauck, *Kirchengeschichte Deutschlands*, II, p. 125, note 1.

(3) Einhard, *Vita Caroli imperatoris*, chap. 25, M. G. H. SS. II. pp. 456-457.

ill brook the intellectual supremacy of their Saxon master; at times, they drove him to seek the protection of Charles from their jealous levity.[1] Nor was this all. Alcuin was wearied by the frequent journeyings of the court, by the excitement of successive wars, and by the care of the abbeys entrusted to his charge. He was discouraged at times by the lack of books, and his righteous soul was vexed by the lax morals of the court.[2]

In view of these circumstances, the Frankish court could have no permanent attraction for Alcuin. He had been practically a recluse in England, was already past middle age, and must have longed for retirement and repose. He sought it in England, whither he returned in 790, probably intending to end his days as the abbot of a small monastery on the banks of the Humber. His hopes were not to be realized; he found himself more than ever embroiled in secular matters. In the first place, he had to act as peacemaker between Charles and Offa, king of Mercia, whose relations with each other had become seriously strained.[3] Upon his arrival at York, he effected a reconciliation between these two potentates,[4] but he found that the political conditions in his native state of Northumbria were such as to preclude all idea of repose or study. Despairing of accomplishing anything in England, he began to think once more of returning to France. Accordingly, when Charles called upon him for aid in combating the heresy of Adoptionism, he set out again for Aachen.[5] This was in 792, and, much as Alcuin loved his native land, he was never destined to return to its shores.

(1) *Carmen*, 42, M. G. H. Poet. Lat. Med. Aev. I. p. 254.
(2) *Vita Alchuini, op. cit.*, chaps. 6, 8. Cf. *Epp.* 121, 80, 244.
(3) *Vita Alchuini, op. cit.*, chaps. 6, 8. Cf. *Epp.* 53, 150, 155, 121, 80.
(4) *Ep.* 244. (5) Cf. Duemmler, *Zur Lebensgeschichte Alchuins, op. cit.* Neues Archiv. Vol. XVIII, p. 63, note 4: Hauck, *op. cit.*, Vol. II, p. 123. *Vita Alchuini, op. cit.*, chap. 6.

After his arrival in Frankland, Alcuin wrote several letters to the leaders of that Adoptionist heresy which he had returned to oppose. Neither these, nor the treatises which he wrote a little later, proved effectual in stemming the tide of heresy. Soon after, however, at the Council of Frankfort in 794, he had the satisfaction of silencing the Bishop of Urgel, one of the chief protagonists of Adoptionism.[1] And it was a source of no little gratification to him that the works which he had written against Adoptionism were used as a weapon by the commission which succeeded in uprooting that 'pestilent' heresy in Spain.[2] Just how much he had to do with the controversy over image-worship which came up at the same Council of Frankfort, is a matter of debate; but it is very probable that he assisted Charles in writing his protests to the Papacy against the doctrine of image-worship.[3]

It was perhaps as a reward for his meritorious services, that Charles made him Abbot of Tours in 796.[4] It is evident that he did not seek this honor. Some time before, indeed, anxious to be entirely free from all further participation in secular affairs, he had requested the king to allow him to retire to Fulda, but Charles set him over Tours in order to reform the monks and re-establish learning there. Here he was destined to spend the remainder of his days, disciplining the monks, administering the great possessions

(1) *Epp.* 73, 23, 207, 208.
(2) "Quos nostra parvitas, quantum potuit, scriptis ecclesiasticis adiuvabat; maxime eo libello, quem nuper edidimus contra libellum illius Felicis." *Ep.* 207. Cf. *Epp.* 208, 200.
(3) As is well known, he brought a memorial against the Nicene Decrees to Charles from the bishops and princes of England. *Annales Nordhumbrani*, M. G. H. SS., *op. cit.*, Vol. XIII, p. 155, note 3. Cf. Hauck, *op. cit.*, Vol. II, pp. 324, 330: Hefele, *Conciliengeschichte*, Vol. III., pp. 651-673.
(4) *Vita Alchuini, op. cit.*, chap. 6. Cf. *Epp.* 101, 247, 121, 143, 172. *Annales Laurissenses Minores*, M. G. H. SS. I, p. 119.

of the abbey, teaching in the school[1] and writing to his friends when his multifarious duties permitted.

In the meantime, events were happening on the continent which gave Alcuin an excellent opportunity for the exercise of his self-imposed task of mentor. In the first place, the crusade against the heresy of Adoptionism, begun at the Councils of Narbonne, Ratisbon and Frankfort, was still being vigorously prosecuted in Spain by a commission which Charles had appointed for that purpose. Alcuin became the head and centre of the attack upon this heresy. Such leaders of the orthodox party as Leidrad of Lyons, Nefridius of Narbonne, and Benedict of Aniane sought the aid of his counsel and of his pen.[2] Then the attack of the Roman mob upon Pope Leo III roused him, and he called upon Charles to aid the Pope and chastise his enemies.[3] Furthermore, there was the coronation of Charles as emperor. Alcuin wrote congratulating him upon his accession to the imperial dignity, and offered as a worthy tribute 'to the new imperial power' a beautiful copy of the Gospels.[4]

Not a little of Alcuin's time at Tours was spent in writing commentaries on the Bible. In addition to the revision of the Scriptures which he prepared at Charles' request,[5] he commented upon a number of the books, both of the Old and New Testament.[6] Thus, teaching, writing, cor-

---

(1) Duemmler, *Zur Lebensgeschichte Alcuins, op. cit.*, Neues Archiv. Vol. XVIII, p. 67. Cf. *Vita Alchuini, op. cit.*, chap. 8. Cf. *Epp.* 101, 247, 146, 150.

(2) *Epp.* 149, 207, 208.

(3) *Ep.* 174. Cf. *Ep.* 179, wherein he exhorts his friend Arno to champion the Pope's cause.

(4) "Sed quaerenti mihi et consideranti nihil dignius pacatissimo honori vestro inveniri posse [videbatur] quam divinorum munera librorum." *Ep.* 261. Cf. *Epp.* 262, 217.

(5) "Totius forsitan evangelii expositionem direxerim vobis, si me non occupasset domni regis praeceptum in emendatione veteris novique testamenti." *Ep.* 195. Cf. *Epp.* 196, 209, 213, 214.

(6) *Epp.* 261, 262. Cf. *Vita Alchuini, op. cit.*, chap. 12.

responding, did Alcuin spend many useful, happy hours; and we can readily believe that he would fain have employed all his time in this way; he never speaks with pleasure of the broad acres which his abbey ruled and owned, though he delighted in dispensing his hospitality to the numerous guests who were attracted there by reason of its wealth and its reputation.[1] However, with advancing age, the secular duties which his office entailed proved more and more irksome to him. "We are well-nigh overwhelmed by the burden of worldly affairs and the responsibilities of wealth," he writes to Arno.[2] Other letters written at this stage of his career are eloquent of his desire to have done with the active affairs of this world. Sickness and feebleness oppressed him and he longed for rest.[3] Even the kind attentions of the king failed to rouse him; and though the latter tried to induce him to visit the palace, he preferred to remain amid the 'smoky roofs of Tours.' In a touching letter to Charlemagne, he plead with him to be allowed to retire, and when his request was granted, he expressed his satisfaction again and again to his most intimate friends.[4]

Unfortunately, the peaceful close which Alcuin contemplated was not yet to be his, for a most unhappy quarrel with his friend Theodulph, Bishop of Orleans, came to sadden his last days. It seems that Alcuin gave asylum to a certain delinquent whom Theodulph had tried and imprisoned. A quarrel ensued, and both of them appealed to Charles. To Alcuin's great sorrow, the emperor not only sided with Theodulph, but, angered at Alcuin's temerity in opposing his authority, cast aspersions on the monks of St. Martin's, even hinting that Alcuin's disci-

---

(1) On one occasion in 800 A. D., Charles honored him with a visit. *Ep.* 165.   (2) *Epp.* 53, 150, 156, 159, 167, 70, 113.
(3) *Epp.* 192, 229, 238, 253, 254, 240, 266.
(4) *Epp.* 178, 170. Cf. *Epp.* 237, 233, 234, 235, 239, 240.

pline must have been lax.[1] However, it is pleasing to note
that Charles forgave him, partially at least, and cheered
his declining years with some marks of his favor. The
former intimacy was renewed; Charles wrote asking for
explanations of his difficulties in theology and astronomy, and Alcuin showed his keen appreciation by
dedicating to him most of his exegetical works written at
that time.[2] Furthermore, agreeable to Alcuin's wish, the
emperor appointed Fridugis as his successor, and invited
Alcuin himself again and again to the court. These invi-
tations were humbly but firmly declined, the old scholar
pleading the infirmities of age.[3] A little later, a year or
more before his death, he took a dignified and pathetic farewell of Charles, thanking him for all his kindness and re-
minding him of the importance of preparing for death and
the judgment. About the same time he wrote to Pope Leo
III, asking him to pardon his sins.[4] As he neared the end
of life, he was filled with a strange dread of death. "I
tremble with terror at the thought of the Judgment Day,"
says he, "lest it find me unprepared."[5] He expressed a
desire that he might die on Pentecost, and yearned
with an intense longing to be buried by the side of St.
Boniface at Fulda. He was far too weak to admit of his
being taken to Fulda; but part of his wish was fulfilled,
for his life went out in a beautiful close just as the matins
had been sung on Whitsunday, May 19th, 804 A. D.[6]

(1) When Theodulph demanded that the delinquent be delivered
into his hands, he seems to have been acting as a *missus* of the king.
Ep. 247. Cf. *Epp.* 245, 249.
(2) *Epp.* 257, 261, 306, 136, 304. Cf. *Ep.* 242, edition of Jaffé.
(3) *Epp.* 178, 238, 239, 240, 241.
(4) *Epp.* 234, 238.
(5) *Epp.* 239, 252, 242, 266.
(6) *Vita Alchuini, op. cit.,* chaps. 14, 15. *Ad Annales Petavianos,*
M. G. H. SS., Vol. III, p. 170.

CHAPTER I

ALCUIN'S THEOLOGICAL RÔLE

To the historian of dogma, the Carolingian Age does not offer much, unless he wishes to study the appropriation of old and familiar material rather than the evolution of new doctrines. For the first creative period of Christianity, after it had come under the influence of Greek philosophy, was much anterior to that age; nor had it yet entered upon its second phase, scholasticism. The philosophy and theology of the patristic period, handed down in part through compendia, was being propagated in new abridgments. Those who wished to attain to the highest theological culture read Augustine and the other Latin fathers; but very few scholars of the Carolingian Age went back of Gregory the Great and Isidore of Seville, and none of them, with the possible exception of Johannes Scotus, was able to probe that patristic intellectual world in its deeper ideas and perceptions and make it a part of their own experience.[1]

Thus we need look for nothing new in the theology of Alcuin's period; deeply distrustful of itself, slavish in its adherence to authority, it gropes after the traditions of the past; yet it is not without interest, owing to its tendency to mysticism on the one hand, and to materialistic for-

(1) Harnack, *History of Dogma,* translation by N. Buchanan, Vol. V, p. 275. Cf. Ueberweg, *History of Philosophy from Thales to Present Time,* translation by George Morris, Vol. I, p. 355. Hatch, *Introductory Lecture on the Study of Ecclesiastical History,* 1885.

malism on the other. These were so much in harmony with the spirit of the age and so insidious in their influence as to have been either unnoted by the most enlightened men of the day, or, if so, to have been viewed without distrust and even with equanimity. In matters of practice, there had long been a tendency to formalism which was marked by a steady decline of religion into a ceremonial service, and a belief in the miraculous. The growing influence of Rome over the west in matters of faith and practice, furthered as it was by the ecclesiastical reforms of Charles the Great, was a very potent factor in promoting uniformity and formalism as well as orthodoxy; while the tendency to mysticism combined with the woful ignorance and superstition which characterized the people of the day, will account in a large measure for their inveterate love of the miraculous.

Alcuin shares the tendencies of his age. Like his contemporaries, and his predecessors for several centuries, he is but an echo of preceding writers; he knew no philosophy, no theology save what he found in the Church Fathers, or in an allegorically interpreted Bible. He makes this very clear in a letter to Gisla and Rodtruda[1] wherein he explains that, as a physician doth compound out of many drugs and herbs a specific for the healing of the sick, so he himself, for the spiritual upbuilding of the faithful, doth glean truths from the Fathers as 'veritable flowers of the field.'[2] Nor does he presume to trust his own judgment. "Rather," says he, "have I been careful to follow the beaten path of the Fathers, imploring the aid of Divine Providence that I might interpret their meaning aright."[3]

Alcuin's theological works may be roughly classified as

(1) Sister and daughter, respectively, of Charles the Great.
(2) "Florida rura peragranda mihi esse video." *Ep.* 213, p. 357.
(3) "Magis horum omnium sensibus ac verbis utens, quam meae quicquam praesumptioni committens." *Ibid.*

exegetical, moral, liturgical and dogmatic.[1] In a large measure, they were called forth by the exigencies of the time. This is especially true of the liturgical and dogmatic works; they are quasi-official in character, the former having been written to further Charles' plan of making the liturgy of Frankland conform to that of Rome, and the latter to defend the orthodox church against heresy. Of all his theological works, the dogmatic are certainly the ablest and possibly the most important. These consist of three treatises[2] and of a number of letters, all of them written against the heresy of Adoptionism and its leaders, Felix of Urgel and Elipand of Toledo. They evince a directness and force not found in his other works; possibly, because Alcuin here found a subject after his own heart, a subject which furnished him with an opportunity for the display of his biblical and patristic lore, as well as for the vindication of his orthodoxy.

From the dogmatic standpoint, the chief importance of Adoptionism lay in the fact that it was really an assertion of a duality in the personality of Christ.[3] According to Alcuin, one of their chief opponents, the Adoptionists maintained the unity of the divine person, but they believed in distinguishing strictly between the divine and the human natures of Christ, asserting that Christ, as God, was the natural, and as man, the adopted, Son of God.[4] That is to say, they maintained that He was born once by natural birth as the Son of God, and again, by a process beginning with baptism and culminating in the resurrection, as the adopted Son of God. Thus they emphasized His humanity;

(1) West's *Alcuin*, appendix, pp. 187, 188.
(2) The *Beati Alcuini Adversus Felicis Haeresin;* the *Beati Alcuini contra Felicem Urgellitanum Episcopum Libri VII,* and the *Adversus Elipandum Tolitanum Libri IV,* in Migne, CCI, pp. 83-299.
(3) Cf. Gaskoin *Alcuin,* p. 140.
(4) "Dicis itaque quod unus homo duos patres naturales non possit habere, et alterum adoptivum," et seq. *Adv. Fel.* Book III, chap. 2. Migne CCI, p. 163: Cf. *Ep.* 23; Harnack *op. cit.* V, pp. 282-285.

Christ was a Son no less in His humanity than in His
divinity; but His nature as the Son of man was different
from that He possessed as the Son of God.   Accordingly,
those who asserted that in His human natures He was
properly and strictly the Son of God, confounded His two
natures and denied that any difference existed between God
and man, the Word and the flesh, the Creator and the
creature.[1]

The origin of Adoptionism has long been a disputed
point.   It does not lie within our province to discuss it.[2]
Suffice it to say, that the term Adoption had lingered on
from early times in the Spanish Church, where it had been
perpetuated by some passages in the so-called Mozarabic
liturgy.   It did not become a burning question in Spain
until its chief protagonist, Elipand, Bishop of Toledo, tried
to subject the province of Asturias to his ecclesiastical
jurisdiction.[3]   It became a matter of great moment to the
whole of Western Europe, when Felix, Bishop of Urgel,
came forward as its champion.   Now, Felix's diocese lay
within the borders of Frankland, and Charles the Great,
realizing that Felix and his new doctrine were becoming
disturbing factors among his newly conquered people, re-
solved to repress them both.   His first expedient was to
have Adoptionism condemned by the councils of the church.
That proved ineffectual, although Felix was forced to re-
cant at Ratisbon, and Adoptionism was condemned at the
Council of Frankfort.[4]

At this juncture, Alcuin became prominent in the controversy.   He had been received into the Council of Frankfort, and it is possible took part in its deliberations.[5]   How-

(1)   *Adv. Fel.* III, 17; Migne CCI, pp. 171-173.
(2)   Cf. Harnack, *op. cit.* V., pp. 278-283 and footnotes; Hefele, *op.
cit.* III, pp. 642-652; Hauck, *op. cit.* II, p. 290, note 2.
(3)   Moeller, *History of Christian Church*, pp. 130-132.
(4)   Hefele, *op. cit.* III, pp. 661, 671, 678.
(5)   *Annales Einhardi*, M. G. H. SS. I., p. 351.

ever, it was not until it had become apparent that the councils had failed in their purpose that Alcuin would seem to have been singled out by King Charles to champion the orthodox faith. Not long after the Council of Frankfort, Alcuin wrote to Felix adjuring him to renounce his errors. Failing to convince him, he wrote a tract against him.[1] This was followed somewhat later by his larger work against Felix, the *Adversus Felicem*,[2] as well as by his tract against Elipand.

In these works, Alcuin drew largely upon his patristic knowledge and taxed his ingenuity to the utmost in his effort to refute the Adoptionists. In the first place, he strove to crush his opponents by the sheer weight of tradition, declaring that their doctrine was an innovation,[3] without authority in the Scriptures, the Fathers, the decrees of councils, or the practices of the Roman Church. "Why," he asks Felix, "why do you wish to impose a new name upon the church? Has God revealed it unto you, amid the Spanish mountains, during these latter days of the faith? Think you that, in contravention to the apostolic teaching and that of the Fathers, you shall be permitted to rear a new church in a remote corner of the earth?"[4] And Alcuin goes on to state that the Fathers of the Church, the Prophets, Apostles and Evangelists, the Angels at the Nativity, as well as the Angel of the Annunciation, nay, the Father himself, on the occasion of Christ's baptism and

(1) The *Beati Alcuini adversus. Felicis Haeresin*, mentioned in *Ep.* 172 and 145. *Cf Adv. Fel., op. cit.* II, chap. 2, Migne CCI, pp. 154-155.
(2) The *Beati Alcuini contra Felicem Urgellitanum Episcopum Libri VII*, written between the years 798 and 799, and approved by the bishops and the King after the Synod of Aachen. Cf. *Epp.* 172, 202, 207.
(3) *Epp.* 23, 166, 193. Cf. *Adv. Elip., op. cit.* IV, bk. 2, chap. I. Migne CCI, p. 256. Cf. *Adv. Fel., op. cit.* I, chap. 1, *Ibid.*, pp. 127-129.
(4) Cf. *Adv. Fel. op. cit.* I, chap. 2. Migne CCI, p. 129. Cf. *Adv. Fel. op. cit.* II, chap. 5, Ibid., p. 150. Cf. *Epp.* 23, 166.

transfiguration, one and all have borne testimony to the
divinity of Christ from the very moment of His conception. Surely no man in his right senses would gainsay the
authority of these doctors of the Holy Catholic Church;
and most assuredly none save the most presumptuous
would contradict the testimony of Holy Writ.[1] On the
other hand, what had the Adoptionists to offset this testimony save their own opinions, together with several
phrases of the Mozarabic liturgy, and a few citations of
doubtful authority from certain Spanish writers?[2] Where
fore, he implores Felix and his friends to abjure that con-
tentious obstinacy which converts error into heresy.[3]

If his opponents are not overwhelmed by such a cloud of
witnesses, Alcuin is prepared to prove, not alone that the
arguments with which they support their contention are
inconsistent and unsound, but that their doctrine of Adoptionism is but the ancient heresy of Nestorianism in a new
guise.[4] Furthermore, he declares that the Adoptionist doctrine in regard to the Incarnation is most degrading to
Christ, and subversive of the faith, in that it ascribes to
Him a servile condition reducing Him to the level of man-
kind.[5] Accordingly, he arraigns the Adoptionists for their
presumption in attempting to search out the hidden mysteries of God, and to set a limit to the Divine Omnipotence.

(1) "Si tantum hominis, reclamant tibi apostoli, reclamant prophetae
reclamat denique ipse, per quem facta est conceptio, Spiritus sanctus.
Obruitur impudentissimum os tuum cunctis divinorum apicum testi-
moniis; obruitur sacris voluminibus sanctis testibus; obruitur denique
ipso Dei Evangelio." *Adv. Fel.* II, 3. Migne CCI, p. 148. Cf. *ibid.*,
infra caps. 7, 13, 16, 17, 18, 19, 20.

(2) "Sed post haec veritatis testimonia novum nomen Dei Filio
cum paucis, Hispaniæ, non dico doctoribus, sed vertitatis desertoribus,
imponere praesumis." *Adv. Fel.* II, 3, *Ibid.*, p. 148. Cf. "Nisi forte et
eorum dicta sicut et in caeteris solebas, depravaris,"—*ibid.*, bk. 7,
chap. 13, Migne CCI, p. 226.

(3) "Non est hereticus, nisi ex contentione." *Ep.* 23.

(4) *Adv. Fel. op. cit.*, III, 1-2; I, 12; II, 2; I, 13; III, 7; V, 3;
III, 2, 3; I, 1; IV, 5; VII, 11; VII, 2, 9; *Adv. Elip., op. cit.* IV, 5;
Ep. 23.

(5) *Adv. Fel., op. cit.* IV, 9; VI, 1, 2.

The Catholic Church of the West was hardly in a position to understand, much less to favor, the view of the Adoptionists. The latter, by emphasizing the humanity of Christ, had demonstrated a way whereby the man Christ could be apprehended as man and as intercessor. This did not appeal to Alcuin and his contemporaries, partly because it was an "innovation,"[1] partly because they had no appreciation of the humanity of Christ. Deeply inoculated with the mysticism of the Greeks,[2] they saw everywhere the mystery of deification; and as was inevitable, orthodox churchmen soon ceased to regard Him in any sense as a human being.

While the controversy was at its height, Alcuin was most indefatigable in his efforts against Adoptionism. He first of all tried to refute its able champion, Felix, whom he adjured to renounce his error, lest after a life of piety, self-sacrifice and devotion, he should endanger the unity of Mother Church and his own soul's salvation.[3] His appeal was in vain. Felix persisted in his heresy, and won so many converts that the Church was put upon the defensive. Alcuin was somewhat despondent; his letters of this period give evidence of a rancor and bitterness which we should hardly have expected in a man of his temperament. He girded himself manfully for combat with the old dragon of heresy, which was once more raising its envenomed head amid the briars and caves of Spain.[4] Soon after the Council of Frankfort, he wrote his first tract against Felix, and sent it by his friend, Benedict of Aniane, to the monks of Gothia to warn them against Felix. The latter was contumacious enough to write a reply, containing, according to Alcuin, worse heresies and more blasphemies than those in his pre-

---

(1) *Epp.* 23, 166.   (2) Harnack, *op. cit.*, p. 289.
(3) Alcuin speaks of him as a man of blameless life and remarkable sanctity. *Epp.* 23, 166.
(4) "Nunc iterum antiquus serpens de dumis Hispanici ruris, et de speluncis, venenatae perfidiæ contritum, non Herculea sed evangelica clava, caput relevare conatur." *Ep.* 139. Cf. *Epp.* 137, 148.

vious works. "Truly," says Alcuin, "the tract ought to be answered since it asserts that Christ is not the true Son of God."[1] His suggestion met with the approval of the king, and he was commissioned to write a second tract against Felix. At his request, Paulinus of Aquila, and others, were to co-operate with him. And it appears that he and Paulinus carried out their part of the program.[2] These polemics, however, were no more effectual against Felix than previous ones had been.

The next move of the orthodox party was to inveigle Felix into a debate before King Charles in open court. In an evil hour, he allowed Leidrad of Lyons to persuade him to appear at the Palace in defense of his cause.[3] His opponent was Alcuin; in the disputation which ensued, the latter's triumph was complete. Felix, awed by his isolation in the presence of his enemies and borne down by the arguments of his foe, at last abjured his error. Later he wrote a profession of the Catholic faith for his clergy, and became reconciled with Alcuin and to the Church.[4]

Alcuin next turned his attention to Elipand, who had remained obdurate and defiant in spite of Felix's recantation. As early as July, 799, Alcuin had written him, imploring him to renounce his innovations and to use his good offices in reclaiming the Bishop of Urgel from error.[5] Elipand's reply was abusive in the extreme. He addressed Alcuin as "a servant of anti-Christ, begotten of the devil, all reeking with the sulphurous fumes of the pit."[6] Thereupon, Alcuin

(1) *Ep.* 148.
(2) Paulinus wrote the *Contra Felicem Urgellitanum Episcopum Libri tres,* Migne XCIX, pp. 343-468. Alcuin mentions this in *Ep.* 208. Cf. *Ep.* 148, p. 241.
(3) *Vita Alcuini op cit.,* chap. 7. Cf. *Epp.* 193, 194, 208 *Adv. Elip.,* bk. 1, chap. 16. Migne CCI, pp. 299, 304.
(4) *Epp.* 207, 208, 199. Yet his recantation was either forced or insincere. Agobard declared that Felix still believed in Adoptionism at the time of his death. *Liber Adversus Felicem,* bk. 1. Migne CIV, p. 33.
(5) *Ep.* 166.   (6) *Epp.* 182, 183.

wrote his *Adversus Elipandum* against his fiery opponent. This, together with his letter to Elipand and his *Adversus Felicem,* he dedicated and sent to the commission which had been appointed to teach and preach against Adoptionism.[1] Supplied with such a wealth of literature, armed with the authority of the Emperor, and blessed by the Pope, the commission of which we have just made mention had every reason to hope for success. And succeed they did. Alcuin proudly boasted that twenty thousand people, bishops, priests, monks, and laymen, had abjured their error, and returned to the bosom of Mother Church.[2] Thus did orthodoxy triumph, yet the struggle had all but exhausted the resources of the Church and had taxed its scholarship to the utmost.

During the Adoptionist struggle, the Frankish church, the Frankish king, and the Pope had worked in unison to effect the extirpation of a heresy which not only interfered with their work of organization, but also ran counter to the spirit of the times. The other controversies of our period did not have the same tendencies, nor was there the same co-operation between the papacy on the one hand, and the Frankish church and King Charles on the other. On two occasions, at least, the latter lagged behind their guides. They rejected image-worship and supported the *filioque.* The last-mentioned doctrine was peculiar to the Latin fathers, having originated in the Augustinian theology.[3] It had been inserted in the Spanish creed, whence it had come to the Frankish kingdom, though opinions differed as to whether it should be inserted in the symbol which had by

(1) The commission consisted of Leidrad of Lyons, Nefrid of Narbonne, Benedict of Aniane. *Ep.* 200.
(2) *Ep.* 208.
(3) Cf. Augustine's *De Trinitate,* IV. 20-Migne, Vol. XLII, pp. 906-909.

degrees obtained in the Frankish church.[1]   Charles was in
favor of so doing, as were also Alcuin and Theodulph.[2]
And at the Council of Aix-la-Chapelle in 809, the Frankish
church decreed that the *filioque* belonged to the symbol.

Alcuin was also drawn into the third controversy of the
period—that over Image-worship.   While it cannot be established that Alcuin was one of the authors of the *Libri
Carolini*,[3] it does not seem unlikely that he assisted in the
writing of this famous refutation of image-worship.[4]   Certainly he was present at the Council of Frankfort where the
Nicene decrees were condemned.   It is equally certain that
while he was in Northumbria he received a copy of the
Nicene decrees relating to image-worship, together with a
request that he draw up a refutation and bring it with him
indorsed by the authority of the princes and bishops of his
country.   Alcuin complied with the king's wishes.[5]   Furthermore, according to some historians, it was upon this work
that Charles and his theologians based their memorial.[6]
This, however, cannot be proved with the evidence at hand.

So far as the controversy itself was concerned, the most

(1)   Gieseler, *Ecclesiastical History*, translated by Davidson, Vol.
II, p. 277, and authorities there cited.
(2)   Cf. Alcuin's *Liber de processione Spiriti Sancti*, Migne CCI,
pp. 63-83.
(3)   The *Libri Carolini* were composed under Charles' name some
time between September, 789, and September, 791, in opposition to the
Decrees of the seventh council of Nicæa. They are not to be con-
fused with the memorial of 85 chapters, which Angilbert took to
Rome. Cf. *Ep.* 33, Jaffé VI, *op. cit.*, p. 245. For the text, see Migne,
vol. XCVIII, pp. 999-1248. Upon the *Libri Carolini* was based the
Capitulary de Imaginibus, published by the Council of Frankfort in
794. Hauck, *op. cit.*, II, pp. 315-316.
(4)   Cf. Hampe, Neues Archiv., Vol. XXI, p. 86; Jaffé, *op. cit.*, VI,
p. 220 and footnote; Gieseler, *op. cit.*, II, p. 267 (footnote 2) ; Hefele,
op. cit., III, p. 697; Hauck favors Angilbert as the author of the *Libri
Carolini*. Vol. II, p. 316.
(5)   M. G. H. Leges, sect. II, I, p. 78.   Cf. *Simeon Dunelmensis*
ann. 792; Haddon and Stubbs, *Church Councils of Great Britain*, III,
p. 469.
(6)   Hauck, *op. cit.*, II, p. 315 (note 1) ; Hampe, Neues Archiv.,
Vol. XXI, p. 86; Moeller, *op. cit.*, II, p. 127.

remarkable thing was the self-reliance and power evinced by the Frankish church. Affecting an indifference towards images, they contended that no one was bound either to worship or to destroy them. Hence, while they condemned the teaching of the Icondules as superstitious and idolatrous, they deplored the excesses of the Iconoclasts. The chief significance of the whole controversy lies in the fact that the higher and more cultured Frankish clergy were not yet prepared to adopt the worship of images. Though the people and the lower clergy would probably have preferred image-worship, the higher clergy set themselves against this phase of the materialism which was sweeping over the West. What measure of their opposition was due to the desire to advance the political purposes of their king, and what to their conscientious scruples, it would be hard to say. Be that as it may, it is largely due to their efforts that image-worship has never been domesticated thoroughly in the West. There it has remained largely an accessory, whereas in the East it is an expression of religious faith.[1]

The dogmatic works with which we have dealt thus far, make it very evident that Alcuin achieved little in the way of constructive work. However, he wrote one treatise in which he made an effort to evolve a system of theology. This is the *De Fide Sanctae Trinitatis*.[2] Dealing as it does with the Trinity, the Incarnation, the Spirit, and the Resurrection, the *De Fide* is an attempt to give an orderly account of Christianity. Unfortunately for Alcuin's reputation as a theologian, the work is entirely lacking in originality, being based on a treatise of Augustine. Probably the most significant thing about the whole work is the dedication, wherein he declares that one of his objects in writing it is to prove Augustine's dictum, that dialectic is essential to the

(1) Harnack, *op. cit.*, V, pp. 306, 307.
(2) Migne, CCI, pp. 9-63.

proper study of theology.[1]   This, and certain other passages
in his letters, wherein he defends the employment of dialectic
in theological discussions, would seem to foreshadow the
later scholasticism.[2]

The exegetical works of Alcuin are even less original, and
certainly less important, than his dogmatic treatises.   For
the most part, they consist of commentaries on the Bible.
In composing these, his sole aim is 'to cull' the best
thoughts from the earlier commentators, and then to ex-
pand them into one continuous exposition of the passage
under discussion.   It was far from his purpose to lay before
the reader any original ideas about the texts under consideration.   The Fathers are infallible; it is not for him to criti-
cise but to understand the truth as they explain it.   In the
dedication of his commentary on the Gospel of St. John, to
which we have referred, he makes this very clear.[3]   It may
be noted that the first eleven chapters of this same commentary on St. John are taken word for word from that of
Bede on the same subject.   The same plagiarism character-
ises his other works.   His commentary on Genesis is de-
rived partly from Jerome, partly from Augustine; that on
the Penitential Psalms, as he himself avows, is little more
than a reproduction of the expositions of Augustine and
Cassiodorus.   The commentary on Ecclesiastes was based
on Jerome; and his exposition of the epistles of Titus and
Philemon are a reproduction of a similar work by the same
Father.   The commentary on the Songs of Solomon is de-
rived from Bede.   For his work on the Epistle to the
Hebrews, he obtained most of his material from Chrysostom
(in a Latin version).   For the Apocalypse, he drew heavily

(1)   For the content of the *De Fide Sanctae Trinitatis,* see Gaskoin,
Alcuin, pp. 159-163.
(2)   Cf. "Beatum Paulum legimus cum Stoicis disputare, ut eorum
eos disciplinis ab errore in viam veritatis transduceret," et seq. *Ep.* 307,
p. 470.   Cf. *Ep.* 136, and *Grammatica,* Migne CCl, p. 854.
(3)   *Ep.* 213, p. 357.

from Bede, Ambrose, Jerome and Augustine. In his exegesis of St. Matthew, he departs to some extent from his method of excerpting; he expresses his own ideas occasionally, though oftener than not he is satisfied with rearranging the homilies of Bede on the same subject.[1]

All of these commentaries are practical manuals or catechisms, designed to aid his pupils in their own spiritual progress or in the practical work of preaching. His interpretation is three-fold—literal, allegorical, and moral. In connection with the second of these he gives free rein to his fancy; and is particularly fond of elaborating the mysteries of numbers.[2] Sometimes also, as in the case of the commentary on Genesis, he throws his exposition into the form of a dialogue.[3]

Alcuin's exegesis pursues the well-beaten path of allegory which had been followed by the earliest Fathers in their attempts to reconcile the Old Testament with the Gospels. In this respect, the northern imagination, bred amid the lingering myths and legends of Anglo-Saxon barbarism, showed itself to be almost the equal of the long-trained Greek intellects of Alexandria. In the old Saxon literature, every thought assumed a form, every emotion found expression, the forces of evil took on tangible shape. Their imagination conjured up a fantastic people—dwarfs, giants, valkyries; stronger, cleverer than men and lying in wait for their souls. Alcuin's works were full of such allegorical figures. According to his biographer, Alcuin himself came into contact with the devil. "He awoke in the night," says the anonymous writer of the *Vita*, "the door of his cell opened, and he saw the terrible form of the evil one come

(1) Cf. Monnier, *Alcuin.* pp. 206-208; Hauck, *op. cit.*, II, p. 137; Mullinger, *The Schools of Charles the Great*, p. 90; Gaskoin, *Alcuin, op. cit.*, p. 135.
(2) See Chap. 3, p. 90.   (3) Migne, CC, p. 515, *et seq.*

stalking through."[1] He gives the old fantastic time-honored interpretations to various passages of Scripture. Thus, the 'seven eyes' mentioned in Revelations, chapter v, verse 6, he thinks may refer to the Fathers of the church who have illuminated it with the light of their knowledge.[2] And the word *abyss,* so often encountered in Holy Writ, he explained as the 'waste of waters,' 'the heart of man,' 'the ineffable wisdom of God.'[3] Moreover, in one of the least important of his works, *Interpretationes Nominum Hebraicorum,* starting from the assumption that Christ was descended from all the patriarchs, he concluded that the mere enumeration of these ought to incite the faithful to virtue. Accordingly, he proceeded to mention the names of the Old Testament worthies; and along with them he gave a literal, moral and allegorical interpretation of each name.[4]

Likewise, in attempting to explain the passages of Scripture relating to the two swords,[5] he gives another example of his three-fold interpretation. The epistle in which he does so is written to Charlemagne, and is well worth some consideration in view of the fact that it suggests the mental attitude and foreshadows the method of the later scholastics. Thus, he first states the problem, the *nodus vero propositae quaestionis,* as he expresses it. This is none other than to harmonize two passages of Scripture seemingly incongruous and irreconcilable. To render the problem more difficult and so to add more zest to its solution, he quotes four other relevant passages.[6] The result is a Gordian knot impossible of solution to any less skilled than Alcuin himself. "If the sword is the Word of God," says Alcuin, "and the Lord used it in that sense when He commanded His disciples to

(1) *Vita Alchuini, op. cit.,* chap. 13.
(2) *Commentarium in Apocalypsin,* bk. 1, Migne CC, p. 1098.
(3) *Ep.* 38.
(4) Migne CC, pp. 723-729.
(5) Luke xxii, 36; Matt. xxvi, 52.
(6) Eph. vi, 17; Luke xxii, 38; Luke xxii, 50; John xviii, 10.

buy it, then it follows that those who receive the Word of God shall perish by that same Word; for, did not Christ himself say "For all they that take the sword shall perish with the sword'?"[1]

Having stated his problem, Alcuin proceeds to the literal interpretation. "We must bear in mind," says he, "that 'sword' has many possible interpretations, such as the 'passion of Christ,' or 'division,' or 'vengeance,' 'judgment' or 'the Word of God.' "[2] Thus with wearying prolixity and far-fetched analogies, he wanders with keen enjoyment from one irrelevant quotation to another. Finally, having disposed of these men of straw, he comes back to the problem in hand—the reconciliation of the above passages. He states as a premise for the solution of the problem, that sword has always been used in these passages with a two-fold meaning. Following the interpretation of the Holy Fathers, lest his own "may seem presumptuous,"[3] he explains that "sword" is used in one of two senses, signifying, first, "the Word of God," and, second, "an instrument of vengeance."[4]

Then follow the allegorical and moral interpretations. Thus, the "two swords" may refer to the body and the soul. These co-operate through faith; for the latter, latent in the soul, showeth itself outwardly in works. Hence, also, the "two swords" may not inaptly be interpreted as faith and works. This interpretation gives him an opportunity to point his moral. "Let each one," says Alcuin, "look to the secret intents of his soul, and see to it that he bring forth good works. Let the priests be shining lights to their people, feeding them on the Bread of Life. Above all, let those in high places in the church labor through faith and good

(1) Eph. vi, 17; Matt. xxvi, 52.
(2) Cf. Luke ii, 35; Matt. x, 34; Romans xiii, 4; Isaiah xxxiv, 5; Deut. xxxii, 41; Eph. vi, 17.
(3) "Ne quid nostra parvitas praesumptiose dicere videatur." *Ep.* 136, p. 207.   (4) Matt. xxvi, 52; Luke xxii, 51.

works to effect the salvation of their flocks, knowing that those who labor most will reap the greatest reward."[1]

⌐ Thus Alcuin's exegesis is commonly naive and puerile. The commentaries are dull and lifeless, unrelieved by any sudden or agreeable turn, such as meets us in the tracts against Adoptionism. With the exception of a few passages in his commentaries on St. John and on St. Matthew, there is no personal note, no color to relieve the tedium. Furthermore, there is no speculation; nothing in short but an interpretation of the truth as Alcuin saw it through the medium of the Fathers. Yet, his exegetical works exercised a certain influence on his successors. His system of 'culling' from the Fathers served as a model both as to ideal and method for the commentators of the next century. Moreover, he was in some slight measure a precursor of the later scholastics, since there are passages in his works which foreshadow the method and attitude of the later dialecticians.[2]

The moral works of Alcuin have no more claim to recognition as original treatises than his exegetical writings. They are largely based on St. Augustine's works; and we find in them the same ideas and the same manner of treatment. This is very noticeable in the *De Animae ratione,* where Augustine's three-fold division of the function of the soul is reproduced. The moral treatises are three in number. The first of these, the *De Virtutibus et Vitiis,* was composed for the use of Count Wido.[3] It begins in a characteristic way by asserting that obedience to God is the only true wisdom. The second work, the *De Animae ratione,*[4] deals with a kindred subject; it is dedicated to Gundrada or Eulalia. "The love of God," he says to the latter, "is

(1) *Ep.* 136.
(2) Cf. his *Dialectica* and introduction to *De Fide Sanctae Trinitatis.* Cf. *Epp.* 136, 307.
(3) Migne, CCI, pp. 613-639. (4) *Ibid.,* pp. 639-649. *Ep.* 309.

the highest good. Your chief duty consists in loving this same highest good, and you will attain to excellence only in so far as the love of God is implanted in your soul. For it is rational to love one's neighbor, the soul itself, and the body.[1] The passions which would else overturn and destroy this order are to be controlled if not suppressed by the four cardinal virtues." So far as the origin of the soul is concerned, it remains a mystery known to God alone. Furthermore, it is immaterial, impalpable, and invisible; there are found in it only the functions of understanding, will, and memory.[2]

Alcuin's third moral work was a brief treatise on confession. It was intended as a corrective against a certain indifference among the Franks with respect to the confessional. In a letter to the boys of St. Martin he writes, "All sins are known to God; there is no concealing them; therefore, confess and do penance for your sins. Verily, confession is as medicine to the soul; by it you will foil your adversary, the devil, and save your souls.[3] But if ye will not confess to the priest," he says elsewhere, "neither will ye confess to God. The priest has the power of binding or loosing and of reconciling man with God; but how can his good offices avail those whose sins he knoweth not? Hence," he concludes, "have recourse to the specific of confession, and cleanse thyself with the medicine of penance that thou mayest be saved."[4]

In connection with the moral treatises, the biographical works may be mentioned. In aim and characteristics, they bear a strong resemblance to those with which we have just been dealing. They are four in number, and for the most

---

(1) *Ep.* 309. Cf. Migne CCI, p. 641.

(2) "Si totas non habet, quia haec omnia ad unum charitatis intendunt preceptum, quae sola in catholicae fidei veritate, dignam efficiet animam habitatione sanctae Trinitatis." Migne CCI, p. 646. Cf. *Ep.* 309. *De Trinitate*, X, 12, Migne XLII, p. 984.

(3) *Ep.* 131; Cf. Migne CCI, pp. 649-655. (4) *Ep.* 138.

part are adaptations or abridgments from an earlier biographer.[1] Full of unbounded admiration for the saints whose lives he is depicting, he not only dilates on their heroic careers, their virtues and their sanctity, but he accepts and passes on to posterity a goodly number of unauthenticated miracles and prodigies, which tradition or preceding biographers have ascribed to them.[2] These are modeled for the most part upon the miracles of Christ and of the Apostles. St. Martin and St. Riquier, St. Vedast and St. Willibrord, all have the gift of prophecy and of miraculous power. St. Willibrord, for example, produces from four flasks wine enough to satisfy forty persons. All of these holy men heal the sick, restore the lame, the halt and the blind, and bring the dead back to life. A helpless paralytic recovers health and vigor through the saving grace of St. Willibrord;[3] three dead men, one of them the son of a widowed mother, are restored to their friends by the miraculous power of St. Martin.[4] Nor is the human interest lacking. Alcuin does not fail to appeal to the martial spirit of his age. These same saints, who with self-sacrificing devotion bare their heads to the assassin's sword, upon occasion rise in righteous indignation, and, with the courage of Berserkers, rush into the midst of the heathen, firing their temples or putting them to flight while revelling in some ungodly orgy.[5] Such stories as these aroused the imagination of the Saxon and of the Frank, and incited them to emulation. They subserved Alcuin's purpose, which was to edify rather than to inform; and the result is a homily rather than a biography. In fact, following the biography proper, there invariably comes a homily, wherein the author dilates upon the resplendent virtues and

(1) Gaskoin, *Alcuin, op. cit.,* p. 139.
(2) *De Vita Sancti Martini Turonensis,* chaps. 8, 12—Migne CCI, pp. 657-664.
(3) *Vita Sancti Willibrordi,* chap. 28, Jaffé, *op. cit.,* VI, p. 58.
(4) *Vita S. Martini, op. cit.,* chap. 5, Migne CCI, p. 660.
(5) *Ibid., et infra.*

the godlike deeds of his heroes. As a fitting climax there is an account of the translation of each of the saints to the beatific joys of heaven.[1]

From this short survey of Alcuin's theological works, it is apparent that his predominant characteristic is an exaggerated veneration for the past. Like his contemporaries, he is wofully ignorant when compared with the writers of ancient and of modern times; but he had sense and intelligence enough to perceive his limitations. His feeling of weakness and helplessness created in him a deep distrust which made all original work impossible. For Alcuin and his contemporaries, it was a paramount necessity to defend the faith in that form in which it had been delivered to them by the saints. What the Scriptures taught, what the fathers and the church had sanctioned, that they believed, nothing more, nothing less. Tertullian's *credo ut intelligam* was the basic principle of their spiritual life. Their unquestioned acceptance of tradition was so complete as well-nigh to devitalize faith; for they accepted dogmas without hesitation, and failed to bring them into connection with that religious motive which must inspire spiritual life. Yet there is compensation. For if their theology is formal, utterly lacking in originality or force, their trust is sublime, the sincerity of their faith unmistakable.

(1) St. Willibrord was borne to heaven by angels. "Nam vidisse se testabatur animam sanctissimi Patris sui cum magna luminis claritate, cum consona canentium laude, ab angelicis exercitibus ad coelorum regna portari." Chap. 26, Jaffé, *op cit.*, VI, p. 58.

CHAPTER II

SOCIAL AND POLITICAL CONDITIONS

ALTHOUGH to the theologian the Carolingian Age has little to offer in the way of constructive work, to the historian
of civilization the whole era is interesting. In the earlier
part of the period, during the reign of Charles the Great,
the organization of the Frankish kingdom and church was
being completed. Then, too, as a fitting consummation to
Charles' career of conquest, the Empire was re-established
in the West. Likewise, that other universal power, the
Papacy, under the protection of the Frankish king, was
laying the foundations for its future growth and development. At the same time, there was emerging and develop-
ing the Feudal System, in a sense the enemy of both Church
and State, of Papacy and of Empire. In fact, society was
already taking on many of those characteristics which distinguished it during the Middle Ages.

One of the institutions to which Alcuin devotes considerable attention is the Papacy. As portrayed by him, it was
as yet weak and dependent, but very ambitious. Hadrian
and Leo III, the bishops of Rome, its incumbents during
his time, were aware both of the limitations and the possibilities of the papal power, and pursued a consistent policy
toward the temporal rulers of their time. Beset with foes
in Italy and in Rome itself, deserted by the Eastern Empe-
rors, they saw the absolute need for maintaining the alliance
with the powerful Frankish kings. Yet, with a growing

38

prescience of the dignity and possibilities of their own power, they were quick to seize every vantage point which would increase the prerogatives of the Papal See. And on several occasions, notably during the well-known controversies over Image-Worship and the *filioque,* they upheld the pretensions of the Papacy so persistently as to incur the anger of Charles, thereby endangering the alliance between it and the Frankish kings.

However, circumstances were such as to force the popes of Alcuin's time to cling to the Frankish alliance. The encroachments of the Arian Lombards, together with the popes' uncertain position in Rome itself, had first forced them to appeal for aid to the Frankish kings. The well-known conspiracy of Campulus and Paschalis against Pope Leo III is a case in point. When a rumor reached Alcuin to the effect that a Roman mob had set upon the pope and maltreated him, Alcuin was greatly dismayed and angered. "O, perverse people," he exclaims fiercely, "ye have blinded your own head." And he at once implored Charles to make peace with the Saxons so that he might be able to go to Rome and reinstate the Pope.[1] After Charles had gone to Rome, and the Pope, owing to his good offices, had triumphed over his foes, Alcuin broke forth into a veritable pæan of thanksgiving and praise.[2] But it is most significant that the Pope was restored to his position only after what was practically a trial on charges.[3] Indeed, Alcuin hints that for a time Charles actually contemplated asking Leo to resign.[4] A more humiliating position for the 'Servant of the Servants of God' can hardly be conceived; seldom in all its

(1) *Epp.* 173, 174, 179.
(2) "O dulcissime, decus populi christiani, o defensio ecclesiarum Christi, consolatio vitae praesentis." *Ep.* 177.
(3) It would appear that neither Alcuin nor Charles were sure of Pope Leo's innocence. Cf. *Epp.* 179, 184, 214, 216, 218. *Einhardi Annales,* M. G. H. SS. I, pp. 188-199.
(4) Alcuin dissuaded Charles from so doing. Cf. *Epp.* 178, 179.

existence has the Papacy furnished a more striking example of pitiable dependence upon the temporal power.

Pope Leo realized that his position had been greatly weakened by these events. In his subsequent letters to Charles,[1] he confessed that as God had made the Frankish king the guardian of the ecclesiastical peace, the Pope looked to him not alone to defend the temporality of the Church, but to maintain its spiritual prerogatives as well.[2] On the other hand, he held it to be the duty of the Church to second Charles in all his plans, while he felt it incumbent on himself to communicate to the emperor anything of importance which might affect the imperial power of Italy or throughout the West.[3] Under such circumstances Charles was not likely to resign a single prerogative in favor of the Papacy.[4] There were times when he actually usurped that which the Papacy confidently expected him to protect. In a letter to Pope Leo III, he roughly delimited the respective spheres of influence of the papal and temporal powers as follows. "It is our task," he says, "to protect the Holy Church of Christ from the heathen who assail it abroad, as well as to enforce a recognition of the Catholic faith within our borders. It is your duty, O Holy Father, to support our warlike service with hands uplifted to God, so that the Christian people, led of God and aided by your prayers, may triumph everywhere."[5] Thus, there was little left to the Papacy save the exercise of the purely spiritual functions.[6]

(1) Ten letters in all. Hampe in M. G. H. Epistol. Vol. V, pp. 85-104.

(2) "Ad hoc omnipotens et invisibilis Deus noster vestram a Deo protectam imperialem potentiam sanctae suae ecclesiae fecit esse custodem. . . . *Ep.* 9. M. G. H. Epistol. Vol. V, pp. 100. (3) *Ibid., Epp.* 2, 6, 7, 8, M. G. H. Epist., Vol. V.

(4) Hauck, *Kirchengeschichte Deutschlands, op. cit.,* II, pp. 109, 110.

(5) *Codex Carolinae, Ep.* 10. M. G. H. Epistol. Vol. V, pp. 100. Cf. Introduction to *Admonitio Generalis,* M. G. H. Leg., Sect. II, Vol. I, p. 54.

(6) "A l'Empereur l'action, au Pope la prière." Kleinclausz, *L'Empire Carolingien ses origines et ses transformations,* p. 213.

The great men of Alcuin's day acquiesced in Charles' conception of the relations of the Papacy to the temporal powers. Alcuin, though a firm and loyal friend of the Pope, is
in substantial agreement with the views of Charles. To
him the Pope is the Head of the Church, opening to the
faithful the gates of Paradise; he is the heir of all the
Fathers of the Ages and sitteth in their place; upon his
shoulders their mantle of authority and of power hath
fallen.[1] He is the light of life, the chief ornament of religion, the vicar of the Apostles and the anointed of God.[2]
From these expressions, it is evident that Alcuin is a firm
upholder of the Petrine tradition; in matters of doctrine
the authority of Rome is paramount. Further than this,
however, he does not go; he makes no claim for the Papacy
save that of precedence.[3] On the contrary, recognizing its
dangers and needs, he seeks rather to draw it and the temporal powers together as necessary to each other and to
the Church.[4]

"Power," says Alcuin on one occasion, "is divided between the spiritual and temporal powers; the latter must
be the defenders of the former, and, as such, are instru-
ments of vengeance rending their adversaries and punishing
the wicked for their evil deeds; whereas the spiritual, full
of saving grace and power, doth open the portals of Heaven
to the faithful and doth give joy never ending to the good."[5]
Again, he writes to Charles: "Hitherto, there have been
three powers, pre-eminent above all others. First of all,
there is His Eminence the Pope, the Vicar of Christ, who,

(1) *Ep.* 234. Cf. *Epp.* 94, 127, 125, 137, 117, 179.
(2) "Ecce tu, sanctissime pater, pontifex a Deo electus, vicarius
apostolorum heres patrum, princeps ecclesiae, unius inmaculatae co-
lumbae nutritor. *Ep.* 94. Cf. *Epp.* 27, 125. (3) *Ep.* 242, Jaffé, *op. cit.*,
Cf. *Ep.* 174.
(4) "Illi sint, id est saeculares, defensores vestri, vos intercessores
illorum." Cf. "Divisa est potestas saecularis et potestas spiritalis; illa
portat gladium mortis in manu, haec clavem vitae in lingua." *Ep.* 17.
(5) *Ep.* 17.

though even now most grievously ill-treated, (as we know
from your letter), is wont to rule as the successor of Peter,
the Chief of the Apostles.   In the second place, cometh the
head of the secular powers, the Emperor, who of late, as
everyone knoweth, hath been most impiously deposed by his
own people.   In the third place, there is the royal power, to
which dignity it hath pleased our Lord Jesus Christ to elevate thee, vouchsafing thee more power, more wisdom and
more glory than to the other two potentates."[1]   Elsewhere
he describes the Papacy as the successor to St. Peter, the
heir to a great power, the light of wisdom, the shepherd of
the flock, feeding it upon the bread of life, nurturing it with
the flowers of virtue and the Word of God, bearing His
messages to the people, and interceding with Him for their
sins.[2]   The temporal ruler, on the other hand, is an active,
militant force, enforcing the decrees of the Pope, propagat-
ing Christianity, regulating and disciplining the clergy and
protecting the Church against heretic and heathen.[3]   It is
highly probable that Alcuin's training is partially responsi-
ble for his attitude.   For the Anglo-Saxon monks and clergy,
though zealous adherents of the Roman Church, had allowed
their enthusiasm to find its chief vent in an advocacy of Roman doctrines and Roman liturgy.[4]   They were far from
being a unit in favor of the dominating and immediate influence of the Papacy over the national church in England.[5]
Moreover, the English, though Romanic in religion, were
Teutonic in all things else, in literature, language and law.
So Alcuin may well have inherited such a preference for
national independence and for a strong national church as

(1)   *Ep.* 174.
(2)   "Huius te, excellentissime pater, ut vicarium sanctissimae sedis
agnosco, ita et mirificae potestatis heredem esse fateor." *Ep.* 27.
(3)   *Epp.* 174. Cf. *Epp.* 238, 17, 41, 148.
(4)   Cf Synods of Cloveshoe and Pincanhale, Haddan & Stubbs,
*Councils and Ecclesiastical Documents Relating to Great Britain and
Ireland,* Vol. III, pp. 360, 361, 443.
(5)   Haddan & Stubbs, *Remains,* pp. 208, 209, 223.

to induce him to support Charles in his assumption of supremacy in ecclesiastical matters.

Charles was but reaping the advantages of the ecclesiastical policy of the Merovingians. The latter had practically feudalized the Church, despite its protests and in utter disregard of its canons.[1] During the rule of the first of the mayors of the Palace, the secularization of the Church had gone on at such a pace that the clergy found it all but useless to protest.[2] Boniface himself, the most uncompromising advocate of ecclesiastical privilege, received his archiepiscopal see of Mainz from his royal patrons. It is clear, then, that Charles had the right of investiture both by tradition and by prescription. It is equally evident from the official documents of the time, as well as from the testimony of the clergy themselves, that he used this prerogative to the full.[3] Alcuin undoubtedly received his benefices of St. Loup, of Ferrières and of Tours from the king. Later in life, he had these preferments in mind when he thanked the emperor for all the kindnesses which the latter had shown him.[4] And when, in 803, the emperor conceded to the people and the clergy the right to elect their own bishops, it was a favor granted, not an acknowledgment of a pre-existing privilege.[5]

In other respects, Charles' mastery over the Frankish church is even more evident. He was disposed to regard the disciplining of the clergy as his own special prerogative. In his capitularies, he enumerated their vices, mapped out their line of conduct, berated their negligence, and held them

(1) Cf. Concil. Paris III, ann 557, canon 8, Hefele, *Conciliengeschichte*, III, p. 13. Concil. Paris V, ann 614, canons 2 and 3, *ibid.*, p. 68. Concil. Remens, ann. 625, canon 1, *ibid.*, p. 75. Concil. Cabillon, ann. 644, canon 10, *ibid.*, p. 93.
(2) Hefele, *op. cit.*, III, pp. 518-521.
(3) Altfridi, *Vita S. Liudgeri*, caps. 19, 20, M. G. H. SS. II, pp. 410-411. *Vita S. Bonifatii*, cap. 10, *ibid.*, p. 347. (4) *Ep.* 238.
(5) Lea, *Studies in Church History*, p. 93, and authorities there cited.

up to their duties. It is evident, too, from the letters of the
bishops, that they accepted him as the head of the Frankish
Church. They humiliated themselves, accused themselves
of negligence, and of idleness; they blessed the emperor for
having aroused them from their indifference; they pro-
claimed the necessity of obeying his orders, which, like his
person, they considered as holy.[1] They seemed to have regarded his consecration as king and emperor as having con-
ferred upon him special prerogatives over the Church.[2]
Moreover, it is a well-known fact, that the Councils of the
Frankish Church met at his bidding, discussed the matters
which he put before them, and, what is more, decided them
according to his will. "He issued his rescripts on ecclesiastical matters with fully as much authority as when legislat-
ing on matters purely secular."[3] It is very significant, too,
that contemporaries, including the clergy, should have recog-
nized the king's right to approve the doctrines as well as to
regulate the policy of the Frankish Church. Alcuin, for example, dedicated to him his tract on the Trinity as *the one
best fitted to judge of its merits;*[4] nor did he presume to
publish his larger tract against Felix until Charles had
deemed it worthy to be presented to the clergy.[5] Thus the
Frankish king was complete master of the Frankish Church,
appointing its bishops, disciplining its clergy, confirming its

(1)   *Epistolae Carolinae, Epp.* 26-44. Cf. especially *Epp.* 28, 34, 37,
38, 42, in Jaffé *op. cit.,* IV, pp. 335-430.
(2)   Thus Leidrad in his *Liber de Sacramento Baptismi,* says: "In
quibus quoque verbis notandum est quod post unctionem imo per
unctionem dirigatur spiritus domini in David, sicut in Ecclesia credi-
mus per chrismatis unctionem et manus impositionem dari Spiritum
sanctum." Migne, XCIX, p. 864. Cf. Theodulph, *Ep.* 24, M. G. H.
Epistol. IV, p. 534.
(3)   Hefele, *op. cit.,* II, pp. 678-693 and 721. Cf. Lea, *Studies in
Church History, op. cit.,* p. 62.
(4)   "Neque enim quemquam magis decet vel meliora nosse vel
plura quam imperatorem, cuius doctrina omnibus potest prodesse
subjectis." *Ep.* 257, p. 415.
(5)   *Ep.* 202, p. 335. Cf. *Epp.* 203, 201.

doctrines.[1] For the most part, he used his great power with wisdom and discretion; he directed his efforts along several lines, notably, the revision of the liturgy, the organization of the Frankish clergy, and the reform of their morals and those of the people in general.

The nature and scope of Charles' liturgical reforms were determined by his desire to secure a uniformity in the Church commensurate with that which he was trying to secure in the realm of political affairs. The Frankish Church with its numberless local 'uses' could not be expected to furnish the requisite model. Accordingly, he decided to adopt the Roman use, so that the Frankish and Roman Churches, one in doctrine and in faith, should be one in form and in ritual. The Roman chant, the Roman sacramentary, the Roman calendar and the Roman form of baptism were all to be approved.[2] In carrying out his sweeping policy of reform, Charles was at once confronted by a difficulty. The Frankish uses were in the field; they could not be ousted by a mere command; they must be gradually modified, revised and brought into uniformity with the use of Rome. To execute this task required a man of great tact and ripe scholarship, who, while recognizing the difficulties of the work in hand, and the need for moderation, would yet be in hearty sympathy with its purpose. Such a man was Alcuin.

Alcuin wholly approved of Charles' efforts to make the Frankish liturgy conform to that of Rome. Yet his training and experience had been such as to counsel moderation. In his own land, there had been a struggle between two rival liturgies, and knowing the history of that struggle from the compromise under Theodore of Tarsus to the ultimate tri-

(1) Kleinclausz, *op. cit.*, p. 212. Fustel de Coulanges *Les Transformations de la Royauté*, p. 524.
(2) *Duplex legationis Edictum*, chaps. 23, 24. M. G. H. Leg., Sect. II, I, p. 64.

umph in his own day of the Roman purists at the Councils of Cloveshoe and Pincanhale,[1] he was not likely to be too arbitrary nor too radical in dealing with a similar question in Frankland. This is very evident from a reply to Eanbald, Archbishop of York, who had requested him to compile a new sacramentary. "Have you not an abundance of sacramentaries in the Roman style," says he, "and yet others of a larger size, representing an older use?" "And," adds he, very pertinently, "I would fain have had you teach your clergy something of the Roman Order . . . so that the ecclesiastical ceremonies might be performed in an orderly, respectful way."[2] Manifestly, while Alcuin's love of order led him to prefer the Roman service-books, he was willing to supplement them by the local uses. It was in such a spirit of compromise that he composed the liturgical works ascribed to him.

Alcuin's liturgical works may be classified, first as official, or quasi-official, and second as unofficial. To the first class belong the homiliary, a lectionary and a sacramentary, all designed for use in public worship. About the origin of these, we know all too little. Indeed, it is by no means certain that any copy of the homiliary survives, for the so-called homiliary of Alcuin, printed under his name in the fifteenth and sixteenth centuries, was the work of Paulus Diaconus.[3] Alcuin's homiliary appears to have consisted of two volumes of sermons collected from the Fathers;[4] consequently it filled a long-felt need by thus supplying sermons ready to hand

(1) Haddan and Stubbs, *op. cit.*, III, pp. 367-368.
(2) "Numquid non habes Romano more ordinatos libellos sacratorios abundanter? Habes quoque et veteris consuetudinis sufficienter sacramentaria maiora. Quid opus est nova condere, dum vetera sufficiunt?" *Ep.* 226, p. 370.
(3) Recent researches have discovered a manuscript of the twelfth century, which has on the back of the last leaf of it the inscription "Omilie Alcuini de dominicis per anni circulum et de quibusdam aliis diebus." This would appear to be Alcuin's homiliary. Cf. Gaskoin, *op. cit.*, pp. 222, 223. Morin, *L'homélaire d'Alcuin retrouvé.*
(4) *Vita Alchuini, op. cit.*, chap. 12.

to those of the clergy who were too ignorant to write their own.[1] Alcuin's second liturgical work was the 'companion' or lectionary, which, in its present form, contains two hundred and forty-two epistles for reading on Sundays, fast and holy days.[2] The third and last of Alcuin's official works was the sacramentary. It consisted of the Gregorian sacramentary, followed by a so-called preface and a supplement.[3] Through these liturgical works, and especially through his sacramentary, he did much to restore order in the ceremonies of the church as well as to bring about conformity with the liturgy of Rome.

Besides his official works, Alcuin wrote a number of other treatises on liturgical subjects. Among them is his *Liber Sacramentorum;* it is a collection of masses and was intended for monastic rather than for general use.[4] The same is true of the *De Psalmorum Usu.* This classified the Psalms according to their subject matter, and showed their appropriateness to various moods and circumstances.[5] Another work, the *Officia per Ferias,* or *Breviarium,* as it is sometimes called, was written for Charles the Great himself, or for his son and namesake. It contains a number of Psalms assigned in seven portions, according to their contents, to the seven days of the week; a collect follows every psalm, and there is a litany of saints for each day. Considerable interest attaches to this work in view of the fact that it is said to have brought the word 'brevarium' into general use.[6]

---

(1) *Epp.* 136, 110, 113, 116, 173.
(2) Gaskoin, *op cit.,* pp. 225-231. For the text, see Ranke, E., *Perikopensystem,* appendix, iv-xxvi.
(3) Gaskoin, *op. cit.,* pp. 226-227.
(4) For text, see Migne CCI, pp. 445-466.
(5) Suitable prayers were interspersed throughout the work, and a tabulation of these under fourteen heads concluded the work. *Ibid.,* pp. 465-508.
(6) Alcuin uses the word Breviarium in his introduction: "Quia vos rogastis, ut scriberemus vobis breviarium comatico sermone," et seq. *Ep.* 304. Cf. Migne CCI, p. 509. Batiffol, *History of the Roman Breviary,* p. 205. For text, see Migne, CCI, pp. 509-612.

Along with his liturgical works we may mention his treatise on baptism, written to a priest called Odwin, and designed as a warning to the monks of Septimania against the various malpractices of the Spanish Church, notably the substitution of single for trine immersion.[1] This work, together with those mentioned above, contains the form of worship, both general and special, for ecclesiastical services.

Alcuin's liturgical works, based as they were principally upon the older Roman liturgies, must have greatly aided Charles' plans for establishing ecclesiastical uniformity throughout the Frankish Church. Moreover, though it cannot be very definitely proved, there is some evidence to show that Alcuin played a rôle in carrying out another part of Charles' ecclesiastical program, namely, the revision of the Scriptures. In dedicating his Commentary on the Book of St. John to Gisla and Rodtruda, he writes, "I should have sent you the whole Commentary on St. John, had I not been fully occupied in complying with the king's command to amend the versions of the Old and New Testaments."[2] And again, in one of his carmina he writes: "Receive, O king, this little gift, token of the great love thy Alcuin bears thee. The great ones of earth bring thee precious stones, but I in my poverty bring thee these two little books, lest on that great day I should come empty-handed into thy presence, O most pious and revered king.[3] These I have carefully corrected and bound together in one great volume and have sent them to you through the medium of our very dear son, our faithful servant."[4] Thus there is some ground for accepting the tradition that the Carolingian revision of the Bible was the work of Alcuin.

(1) *Epp.* 134, 137.   (2) *Epp.* 195, 262.
(3) *Carmen,* 65, M. G. H. Poet. Lat. Med. Aev., *op. cit.,* I, p. 283.
(4) *Carmen,* 65, 69, *ibid.,* pp. 283, 284, 288. It appears that three Bibles were revised by him or under his inspection. Cf. Dedicatory Poems, *Carmen,* 65, *ibid.,* I, pp. 283-285.

A large measure of Charles' success in his ecclesiastical reforms was due to the effective control which he exercised over the Frankish clergy. This was made possible in the first place by his assumption of the right to appoint the higher clergy. But his mastery could not be complete until he had effected such an organization as would extend his disciplinary power over every phase of ecclesiastical activity. This was a difficult task to perform. Owing to the interference of the Merovingian kings, the whole church had tended to disintegrate; the system of metropolitans and provincial synods was gradually dying out in western Europe;[1] the diocesan bishops were becoming more and more independent; while the clergy, especially that portion which may be called 'unattached,' were less and less inclined to obey their Bishop. The unattached clergy were very numerous; they served a church which had been founded upon an estate by its owner and were appointed, paid and removed by him; they were thus exempt from outside interference, civil or ecclesiastical.[2] Under such circumstances, discipline was clearly impossible.

Charles the Great sought a remedy. He bent his energies to secure, first, the subordination of the clergy to the bishop in the chief city of their district; second, to co-ordinate the bishops of a province into a single body with the metropolitan at their head; and third, of course, to secure the dependence of the latter upon the royal or imperial power. The administrative machinery, he contemplated, was almost perfect in theory. However, evidences are not lacking to show that it was far from being so in actual practice. In his circular letter to his vassals and administrative officers,

---

(1) Hatch, *op. cit.*, pp. 124-126.
(2) Men sold churches and transferred them. "De Ecclesiis quae ab ingenuis hominibus construuntur; licet eas tradere, vendere. . . ." *Capitulary Francofurt.*, 794 A.D., cap. 54, M. G. H. Leg., *op. cit.*, II, I, p. 78.

Charles complained that some of his clergy had presumed to disobey their bishops, contrary to the laws and the canons, and that some of the priests had been installed in churches without episcopal consent.[1]

As a remedial measure, looking especially to the enforcement of discipline, Charles ordered the priests to report to the bishops once a year, while the latter were also required to visit every priest's church annually.[2] There were three purposes subserved by these visitations. In the first place, it gave the bishops an opportunity to preach—an important duty which they commonly neglected, as is evident from the letters of Alcuin. The latter never lost an opportunity to exhort them to preach, never failed to praise them for so doing, nor forgot to reprove them when they failed in this respect.[3] In the second place, the visitation of the bishop enabled him to check those heretical practices which tended to creep into the administration of the sacraments, especially in those of confirmation and baptism. Alcuin, for example, in view of the heresies of the Spanish Church, deemed it necessary to give the most complete and definite instructions as to how the sacrament of baptism was to be administered to catechumens.[4] The third purpose served was that of discipline. From the time of Charles, the bishop in his tour of visitation acted partly as an officer of the church, partly as an officer of the state. He was commonly invested with power to investigate and adjudge cases of murder, adultery, pagan-worship, and other wrong-doings contrary to the laws of God and man. Indeed, there were times when these

---

(1) M. G. H. Leg., *op. cit.*, II, I, pp. 80, 52-62.
(2) Hatch, *op. cit.*, p. 34.
(3) "Et maxime praedicatores ecclesiae Christi caritatem redemptoris nostri per verba sedulae praedicationis populis ostendant." *Ep.* 136. Cf. *Epp.* 301, 291, 169, 311, 114.
(4) *Ep.* 113. Cf. *Ep.* 68, Jaffé, VI, *op. cit.*

administrative and judicial duties left the bishop little time for his spiritual functions.[1]

Another feature of the organization of the Frankish Church in Alcuin's day was the development of the parochial system. Two sets of causes operated to establish it. The first of these centres around the sacrament of baptism. Owing to the disorganization, incident to the disruption of the Roman empire, the elaborate ceremonial which had once attended the performance of this sacrament had almost died out, inasmuch as it had become increasingly difficult for the catechumens to assemble at one place and at one time, as they had done formerly.[2] Consequently, there was a great lack of uniformity and much irregularity in the administration of this sacrament. Hence it became necessary to restrict preaching at the celebration of the sacraments of baptism, mass and confirmation, to certain churches.[3] These were called 'baptismal' churches, and they naturally obtained precedence and developed into the parish church.

The second cause which contributed to the establishment of the parish was the tithes. The latter, as a Christian institution, would seem to date from the eighth century; they are hardly mentioned during the first seven centuries; the regulations of councils practically ignore them, and there are no civil enactments in regard to them.[4] They came from the state to the church and were originally rents paid for the church lands with which the Frankish kings rewarded

---

(1) "De angustia mentis vestrae pro servitio saeculari adversus sanctitatis vestrae dignitatem, ita ut non liceat melioribus instare officiis, ne animarum gregis Christi lucris inservire." *Ep.* 265.

(2) Hatch, *op. cit.*, pp. 83, 84.

(3) *Concil. Vernense*, c. 7, 755 A.D. Hefele, *op. cit.*, III, p. 589. Cf. *Ep.* 68, Jaffé, VI, p. 316.

(4) The first special mention of them occurs in a letter of Pope Zachary in 748 A.D. Jaffé Regesta, No. 2161. The first civil enactment in regard to them is Charles' *Capitulary Rhispacensia et Frisingensia*, c. 13, M. G. H. Leg., Sect. II, I, p. 228.

their soldiers. It was this which made Charles so anxious to enforce their collection, but this was not his only motive. The fact that they were paid only to the 'baptismal' churches tended to develope the parochial system, and strengthen greatly the episcopal authority. Hence, Charles was particularly desirous that the Saxons and other barbarians should pay tithes, inasmuch as they furnished him with the means of organizing and of supporting the church upon which he relied for help in civilizing these people. However, it is evident from Alcuin's lukewarm support of tithes that they were as yet far from being a fixed tradition in the church. "It may be questioned," says he, "whether tithes were anywhere exacted by the apostles; and if we ourselves, born and bred in the faith, do not care to give tithes, how much more must the fierce barbarians, lately converted, resent their exaction."[1] So far as the latter were concerned, he felt that it would be wise to relinquish them for a time, "even at the expense of the public need."[2]

Alcuin's objection was well taken. The whole ecclesiastical policy of the great king towards the barbarians lacked something of that spirit of moderation which marked his dealings with his own people. He wished to make the bounds of Christendom coterminous with those of his kingdom; in accomplishing this end he was impatient, harsh and unscrupulous in his dealings with the barbarians. Thus, prisoners of war who forswore paganism and accepted baptism, were restored to liberty and freed from tribute; while those who refused to do so were beheaded.[3] Alcuin deplores this policy and ventures to suggest to Charles that he entreat the barbarians gently as "the first fruits of the faith,"

(1) *Ep.* 110, p. 158.
(2) "Quia forte melius est, vel aliquanto spatio ut remittatur publica necessitas, donec fides cordibus radicitus inolescat." *Ep.* 174, p. 289. Cf. *Ep.* 110, p. 158.
(3) *Vita Sturmii*, M. G. H. SS., *op. cit.*, II, p. 376. Cf. *Epp.* 107, 110, 111, 113, and Jaffé, *op. cit.*, VI, *Ep.* 68, pp. 311-318.

teaching them and encouraging them with words of advice and comfort.[1] "If," says he, more boldly, elsewhere, "the same pains had been taken to preach to them the easy yoke and light burden of Christ as has been done to collect tithes, and to punish the slightest infringement of the laws on their part, then they would no longer abhor and repel baptism."[2]

However mistaken Charles' policy towards the barbarians, there can be no question but that he exercised a salutary influence on the Frankish Church in general. Under his impelling genius, the Church of the West acquired, in a large measure, that organization which characterized it during the Middle Ages. The parochial system took shape and form, the jurisdiction of the bishops was extended, and their authority greatly strengthened. The latter, in turn, were subjected to the metropolitan. But the system was not carried to its logical conclusion; for the metropolitans, contrary to the plan of St. Boniface, were the subordinates, not of the Papacy, but of the King and Emperor. The archbishops and the provincial council, except in matters of internal discipline, were superseded by the nation. And the great Frankish Church he had organized was controlled by the national assemblies, to which he summoned laymen and ecclesiastics alike.

The third institution of which Alcuin treats is the Empire. Though there is nothing in his letters that sheds new light upon the circumstances of its founding, they serve well as an illustration of the conception of the empire which obtained in his day. Contemporaries are at one in regarding it as a glorious acquisition of the Frankish kingdom. Alcuin speaks of the "right noble Charles who governed the kingdom of the Franks most gloriously."[3] He and his con-

---

(1) *Ep.* 113.   (2) *Ep.* 111.
(3) "Qui modo cum triumphis maximis et omni dignitate gloriosissime Francorum regit imperium." *Vita Sancti Willibrordi*, cap. 23, Jaffé, *op. cit.*, VI, p. 56. Cf. "Qui regnum Francorum nobiliter am-

temporaries view Charles as king and emperor from the standpoint of the Old Testament ideal. To them he is a prophet-priest, a warrior-king.[1] Chosen of God to lead His faithful people, he is their weapon and defence, their law-giver and judge.[2] Divinely inspired, he uses his marvellous gifts to humble the proud, to defend the lowly and to instruct all his people in the ways of truth, of justice and of virtue. Before his terrible face, the pagans flee in terror; under his overshadowing wing, a Christian people rest in peace. In his hand he holds a conquering sword, from his mouth he proclaims Catholic doctrine.[3] Christianity follows in the wake of his army; he makes the bounds of Christendom coterminous with those of his kingdom and of his empire, and by enlarging both of these he secures peace and safety for his subjects. To these glorious ends, he has been endowed with the government of the Church and of the world.[4] Like unto Joshua, he recalls the people to the worship of the true God by means of his warnings and of his punishments.[5] He is a second David, a mighty prince and ruler, decreeing laws for his people, defending the oppressed, cherishing the foreigner, doing justice to one and all, and enlightening his people with the light of knowledge and of truth.[6] His greatest glory, Alcuin says, consists in this, that he has most earnestly striven to lead the people en-

pliavit." *Vita Caroli*, chap. 31, M. G. H. SS., *op. cit.*, II, p. 460. "Propter dignitatem imperii quam avus regno Francorum adiecerat." *Nithard*, IV, chap. 3, *ibid.*, p. 669. Cf. *Ermoldi Nigelli*, bk. 2 vv. 63, 64, 67, 68, *ibid.*, pp. 479, 480.

(1) *Ep.* 174. Cf. *Epp.* 170, 171, 41, 217, 177.
(2) *Ep.* 174. Cf. *Ep.* 242, Jaffé, VI. Cf. Angilbert, *Carmen*, VI, vv. 63-64, 92. 93. M. G. Poet. Lat. Med. Aev., I, pp. 366-369.
(3) *Epp.* 41, 171, 217. *Ep.* 242 (Jaffé).
(4) *Ep.* 242, Jaffé, VI, p. 779, 780.
(5) *Admonitio Generalis*, M. G. H. Leg., Sect. II, I, p. 54.
(6) "Ita et David olim praecedentis populi rex a Deo electus, et Deo dilectus et egregius psalmista Israheli victrici gladio undique gentes subiciens, legisque Dei eximius praedicator in populi exititit." *Ep.* 41. Cf. *Epp.* 171, 198, 309.

trusted to his care out of the depths of darkness into the great light of the true faith.

When we turn from the Empire itself to the people, we find that the picture which Alcuin presents is a very gloomy one. "The times are perilous," he writes, "tribulation followeth hard upon tribulation; the people are in poverty; the rulers in distress; the church beset with anxiety; its priests in dissension; there is nothing stable; all things are in a state of unrest."[1] Though he penned this letter to Arno in a moment of despondency, it is nevertheless a tolerably accurate picture of social conditions in his day.

The clergy, who were the natural guides of the people, were far from being examples of piety and good-living. The 'true bill' which has been found against them by historians is made out not from the recorded instances of the misconduct of individuals, but is based on the fact of repeated legislation, as well as on the testimony of the most noteworthy contemporaries of that day. In both these sources, the references to the shortcomings of the clergy are clear and incontrovertible. Alcuin complains that they are vain, extravagant in dress, and haughty in bearing, utterly worldly in fact;[2] they listen to plays rather than to the Scriptures; they prefer the 'cithara' to the sweet music of the Psalms.[3] Too ignorant to write their own sermons, they have recourse to homiliaries.[4] They share the worst superstitions of the people, believing in auguries and incantations.[5] It is significant that in writing to Eanbald II, Archbishop of York, he

---

(1) *Ep.* 193.
(2) *Epp.* 20, 40, 66, 114. Cf. Capitulary, *A Sacerdotibus Proposita,* M. G. H. Leg., Sect. II, I, p. 107.   (3) *Ep.* 124.   Cf. *Ep.* 237.
(4) Alcuin condones this practice. Cf. "Quid est omelia nisi praedicatio." *Ep.* 136.
(5) Alcuin himself admits that the Devil sometimes uses these to ensnare those who believe in them. *Ep.* 17. Cf. "*Indiculus Superstitionum et Paganiorum,*" M. G. H. Leg., Sect. II, I, p. 223.

should have admonished him not to let "vain babblings nor scurrilous language proceed out of his mouth."[1]

The capitularies, the acts of church councils, and the regulations of the bishops all contain even more specific charges against the clergy. They accuse the latter of wasting their time in hunting, hawking and feasting.[2] Worse still, they indict them for drunkenness and all manner of lewdness. They assert that some clerics sat up until midnight carousing with their companions; after which some, drunken and gorged, returned to their churches quite unfit to perform the daily and nightly services of the Church, while others, 'straw drunk,' sank down and slept off their debauch in the place of revel.[3] Moreover, devoted as they were to worldly pleasures, the clergy found their duties irksome. They disobeyed their Rule, and neglected their spiritual duties, delegating their pastoral work to vicars, who received the spiritual reward which should have been theirs. Alcuin declared them to be robbers rather than pastors, seeking their own interests rather than those which be of God.[4]

Evidently, the wholesale gifts made to the Church during the seventh and eighth centuries had had a baleful influence upon it. It had become very wealthy. Alcuin himself as abbot of Tours ruled over a vast tract of territory.[5] With the increase of wealth, the Christian ministry became a lucrative profession; simony was rife;[6] the clergy became secularized. Bishops and abbots sought to extend their pos-

---

(1)　*Ep.* 114. Cf. *Ep.* 40.
(2)　*Capit.*, 10, *Karlman*, M. G. H. Leg., Sect. II, I, pp. 24-43.
(3)　M. G. H. Leg., Sect. II, I, pp. 91-99, 107, 440
(4)　"Sint praedicatores, non praedatores." *Ep.* 111. Cf. *Vita Alchuini*, chap. 6.
(5)　Elipand taunts him with having 20,000 slaves. *Ep.* 200.
(6)　"Et hoc praecipue intendite, ut simoniaca heresis funditus subvertatur, quae male dominatur in multis, radicem a iudicibus saeculi sumens, ramos usque ad ecclesiasticas tendens personas . . . pene apostolicam inrepserunt sedem." *Ep.* 258, p. 416.

sessions by encroaching on their weaker vassals. Alcuin himself complained that the abbot of Limoges was trying to exact dues from his monks, over and above those sanctioned by custom.[1] Moreover, it appears that the clergy did not scruple to use the weapon of excommunication as a means of extorting wealth. Charles accused them of buying slaves, *allodia* and other property for themselves and gaining wealth by preying upon the ignorance of rich and poor alike.[2] Under such pastors, it was not strange that the morals of the people became vitiated; that the churches were left without a roof or used as storehouses for hay and provisions, and the altars defiled by birds and dogs.[3]

The evil that men do lives after them, the good is interred with their bones. Hence, Alcuin as a reformer devotes more attention to the moral obliquity of the clergy than to their good qualities. Yet he finds something worthy in the ecclesiastics of his day. His friends Arno, Leidrad, Paulinus, Theodulph and others come in for their share of praise; and he commends the monks of Septimania, of Ireland and of Yarmouth most highly. Of the latter he writes, "It is your greatest glory that you have followed your Rule consistently, both in dress and in all other points of monastic discipline, even as your founder did establish them."[4]

Alcuin's interest lay primarily with the Church and the clergy; he says little of the laity, and that little does not serve to put them in a favorable light. To begin with, the nobles of the court undoubtedly vexed his righteous soul. In a letter to his pupil Nathaniel, he warns him against the ladies of the court, those "crowned doves who fly about the

---

(1) "Dicunt enim; vestri missi mandassent presbiteros nostros; de pane modio I et dimidio; de vino modio I; de annona ad caballos modia quattuor; casios VI; ova C." *Ep.* 298.

(2) *Capitula missorum,* M. G. H. Leg., Sect. II, I, p. 115.

(3) "Vidimus quoque aliquibus in locis neglegenter altaria Dei absque tecto, avium stercoribus vel canum mictu fedata." *Ep.* 136. Cf. Einhard, *Vita Caroli, op. cit.,* chap. 17, M. G. H. SS. II, p. 452.

(4) *Ep.* 284.

palace windows."[1] Likewise, he enjoins the chaste Gundrada to be an example to the other ladies of the court, to
the end that they may keep themselves from falling, and so
remain noble in morals as in birth.[2] Magharius, too, the
wise counsellor of the king, is warned not to let worldly
pleasure or carnal delight impede him in his labors.[3] Even
more pointed is the counsel which he gives to Angilbert, and
to Pippin, king of Italy.[4] To Charlemagne himself he
expatiates on the charms of temperance,[5] and on one occasion, at least, is bold enough to speak of the king's shortcomings. "Behold our Solomon," says he, "resplendent in
his diadem and crowned with virtue; imitate his virtues and
avoid his vices."[6]

The nobles are as venal and as corrupt as they are im-
moral. Alcuin intimates that some of the officials were not
above taking bribes, and subverting justice to their own
ends.[7] He has this in mind when he admonishes Charles
to have wise counsellors about him, pious, God-fearing men,
lovers of truth, not given to covetousness. "Let no one
tarnish your good name by dishonesty," says he, "for the
faults of the servants are often ascribed to the Prince."[8]
Likewise, he urges the judges and princes to rule the people
wisely, and to judge them honestly, being fathers to the
widow and orphans; for in the justice of the prince lieth the
happiness of the people.[9] Theodulph of Orleans is even
more outspoken than Alcuin in this connection. "I have
seen judges," says he, "who were slow to attend to the
duties of their office, though prompt enough to take its re-
wards. Some arrive at the fifth hour, and depart at the
ninth; others, if the third hour sees them on the bench,

(1) *Ep.* 244, p. 392. (2) *Ep.* 241. Cf. *Ep.* 309.
(3) *Ep.* 33. (4) *Epp.* 221, 237, 119.
(5) *De Rhetorica,* Migne CCI, p. 941. (6) *Ep.* 309.
(7) "Neque subiectos tuae potestati iudices permittas per sportulas
vel praemia iudicare." *Ep.* 188. Cf. *Ep.* 217.
(8) *Ep.* 217. (9) *Ep.* 18.

will rise therefrom at the sixth. But if there is a bribe to receive, the same men will be in court before the *prima*."[1] Moreover, where perchance the officials were not actually rapacious or unjust, they were inclined to neglect their 'placita' for the pleasures of the chase.[2] No doubt Charles' *missi* had a strenuous time in enforcing justice throughout the Frankish realm. And it would appear that the more conscientiously they fulfilled their duties, the more unpopular they became.[3]

Yet Alcuin finds something to praise in the laity of his day. There are some honorable, upright men among them, some virtuous women; first and foremost among the latter is the 'noblest of the noble,' the fair Gundrada. She it was who, amid the license of the court, had attained to the enviable reputation of being chaste as no other lady of the day.[4] Among the men are Eric, Duke of Friuli, Gerald of Bavaria, and Megenfrid the Treasurer, all of whom Alcuin finds it in his heart to praise most warmly. Naturally, however, it is his master, Charles the Great, who comes in for most of his attention and adulation. As the life-long friend and trusted counsellor of the king, he had ample opportunity to observe his character, and so well did he do so that Charlemagne stands forth from his pages in all his majesty, a sublime figure, commanding the admiration of the ages. There is a significant lack of legend and of myth in his portrayal. It is a living being that he depicts, a man with great faults notwithstanding his splendid virtues As we see him through the medium of Alcuin, he is a mighty man of war, tireless of energy,

(1) Theodulph, *Versus Contra Judices*, vv, 391-396, M. G. H. Poet. Lat. Med. Aev., *op. cit.*, I, p. 493, et seq.

(2) "Volumus atque jubemus ut comites nostri propter venationem et alia ioca placita sua non dimittant nec ea minuta faciant." *Capitula de Causis Diversis*, M. G. H. Leg., Sect. II, I, p. 135.

(3) *Capitula a missis dominicis ad comites directa*, chap. 5, *ibid.*, I, p. 184.

(4) *Ep.* 309.

quick of thought, prompt to act; in fact, a born leader of
men with a genius for organization and command. Withal,
there is much of the barbarian about him; he is in-
describably fierce towards his foes, ruthless and wantonly
cruel at times. On several occasions, Alcuin finds it necessary to plead with him to be merciful. "Be not forgetful,"
says he, "of the captives which Providence granted thee in
thy victory over the Avars; if it be possible, spare some
of them."[1] Again, he suggests that his lord the king should
vary the clash of arms and the strident peal of the horn,
with the softer notes of music, to the end that the fierce
souls of the warriors might be softened.[2]

While not blind to the faults of his great master, Alcuin,
like the rest of his contemporaries, is dazzled by his genius.
At times he seems to be under a spell, and then he is quite
as extravagant as other contemporaries, whose judgment
is less discriminating than his. In such a mood he pic-
tures Charles as a great Christian emperor, whose piety
shines forth as bright as the rays of the sun.[3] The em-
bodiment of virtue himself, he incites all classes of his
people to deeds of virtue; to the soldiers he teaches skill
in the use of arms, inspiring them with constancy and
courage; the clergy and the people he enjoins to obey
in all humility; his counsellors and judges he leads in the
path of wisdom and justice.[4] Thus does he rule his people,
decreeing laws, defending the oppressed, cherishing the
foreigner, and enlightening his people with truth and
knowledge.[5] "Happy the people," says Alcuin, "over whom
Providence has placed so wise and so pious a ruler, who

(1) *Ep.* 118. (2) *Ep.* 149.
(3) *Ep.* 242 (Jaffé). Cf. Angilbert, *Carmen*, VI, vv. 12-15, M. G.
H. Poet. Lat. Med. Aev., *op cit.,* I, p. 366. Theodulph, *Carmen,* 35, 36,
ibid, pp. 526-528.
(4) *Epp.* 177, 136. Cf. Theodulph, *Ep.* 24, M. G. H. Epistolarum,
IV, p. 534. Also Paulinus Aquila, *Ep.* 43. Migne, XCIX, pp. 508-509.
(5) *Epp.* 229, 177. Cf. Einhard, *Vita, op. cit.,* chap. 21, M. G. H.
SS. II, p. 455.

excelleth all, not alone in majesty and power, but in wisdom and religious zeal as well."[1]   These expressions are repeated, until one feels that Alcuin had some merit as a courtier as well as a scholar.

With immorality and license prevailing among the nobility, we need not look for enlightenment or religious zeal among the lower classes in Frankland. The people gave free reign to their passions, and imitated the vices of the nobility. They were especially given to drunkenness, and prone to deeds of violence and bloodshed.[2] Impoverished by the continual wars of Charles' reign, oppressed by their superiors, lay and ecclesiastical, too brutal to command respect, too ignorant and too helpless to effect any amelioration of their condition, their lot was a hard one. They were being reduced to beggary and even to slavery, as Charles himself admits. "If a poor man," says he, "will not give up his property to a bishop, abbot or count, these make some excuse for getting him into trouble with the courts, or they order him continually on military service until the man surrenders or sells his property."[3] The noblest spirits of the time were alive to the fearful degradation of the people; nor did they fail to express their pity. Nevertheless, there was a good deal of contempt mingled with their sympathy. Thus Alcuin, while enjoining upon the lords the necessity of being just and merciful towards the people, felt that the latter ought to obey a just ruler with thankful hearts. Alcuin expressly repudiated the maxim, 'Vox populi, vox Dei,' maintaining that the voice of the people was the voice of madmen.[4]

Bad as were the social conditions in Frankland, those in England were even worse. Alcuin's account is one long

---

(1) *Epp.* 171, 229, 121.   (2) *Epp.* 246, 249, 119, 18, 121, 58, 172, 150.
(3) *De Rebus Exercitalibus,* M. G. H. Leg., Sect. II, I, p. 165.
(4) "Nec audiendi, qui solent dicere; vox populi, vox Dei. Cum tumultuositas vulgi semper insaniae proxima sit." *Ep.* 132.

chronicle of invasion from without, of schism and disorder
from within. He cries out in despair over the ruin of the
monasteries, over the decline of learning, over the social
and political disorder rampant everywhere. "Lo," he says,
"a pagan people lay waste our shores, pillaging and plunder-
ing at will; the princes and people are rent with dissensions; while learning perishes in our midst."[1] With touching sorrow Alcuin depicts the desecration of the churches.
"Alas," says he, "the Church of St. Cuthbert, so honored
by all the people of Britain, hath been given over wholly to
the pagans for plunder; despoiled of its ornaments, bereft
of its glories, it has been spattered with the blood of its
priests. Verily, if the Holy St. Cuthbert cannot defend
his own in that place where religion was first implanted
in our race, verily there remaineth naught for us to do save
to cry out, 'Spare, O Lord, spare thy people, and give not
thine inheritance unto the heathen, lest they say, where
is the Christians' God?' "[2]

The internal dissensions among the princes and people
of England were even more baleful in their influence than
the devastations of the Norsemen. The political unrest,
which had characterized the Anglo-Saxons before and since
their advent into Britain, was much in evidence in Alcuin's
day. According to his testimony, the English kingdoms
had been most unhappy as to the princes who had been
chosen to rule over them. Everywhere they had declined
in those qualities which had been wont to make them a
blessing to their people and a terror to the enemy.[3] They
were tyrants, not rulers; for they plundered their people
shamelessly.[4] The whole land was a prey to intestine
strife; rival claimants to the throne murdered and pillaged,
regardless of their subjects;[5] nobles warred on nobles, and

(1) *Ep.* 129. (2) *Ep.* 16. Cf. *Ep.* 20.
(3) *Ep.* 130. (4) *Epp.* 16, 9, 109, 115. (5) *Epp.* 109, 127, 128, 122.

oppressed the people; everywhere except in Mercia[1] was black ruin, anarchy and disintegration.

The clergy of England were almost as bad as the nobility. There was no sympathy, no co-operation between the higher ecclesiastics; there was coldness between the archbishops of York and of Canterbury;[2] while between the latter and the lately established archbishopric of Lichfield,[3] there was actual strife. Again, the higher clergy were inclined to take a hand in the political disturbances of the day. Thus the archbishop of York interfered in the dissensions of Northumbria with little credit to himself, and less profit to the church.[4] The bad example set by the nobility, lay and ecclesiastical, had a most deleterious effect upon the lower clergy and the common people. "If," says Alcuin, "there proceeds from the nobility and the clergy, the fountains of faith and truth, naught but turmoil and infidelity, we can expect but little from the people."[5] The clerics are distinguished from the laymen by their tonsure alone; in all things else they are reprehensible as the laity themselves, as vain in dress, as haughty in bearing, as much given to feasting, drinking and such like things.[6] The regular clergy are as bad as the secular; they live in luxury, and devote themselves to worldly enjoyments, being more like laymen than monks; they neglect their Rule, especially that part intended for their edification; as they sit at meat, they prefer to listen to plays instead of having one of their number read from the Scriptures or the

(1) Even Offa, king of Mercia, does not escape Alcuin's censure. *Epp.* 122, 123.
(2) *Epp.* 127, 128.
(3) Eventually the archbishopric of Lichfield was suppressed. *Epp.* 128, 255.
(4) *Ep.* 232. (5) *Ep.* 122.
(6) "Quae magna ex parte diu corrupta viluit et pene laicorum vanitate coaequata est, ita ut tonsura tantummodo discreta videtur; ceterum moribus multa ex parte consimilis, ceu in vestimentorum vanitate et arrogantia et conviviorum superfluitate et aliis rebus." *Ep.* 230. Cf. *Ep.* 129.

Fathers, as their Rule commands.[1] As might be expected, the people are much harmed by such conduct; they follow not in the footsteps of their fathers; neither in dress nor in good living do they pattern themselves after their worthy ancestors; but in their mad folly, they seek out some new thing as unprofitable to themselves as it is displeasing to God.[2] "A time of great tribulation has come over our land" wails he, "the faith is losing ground; God's truth is not spoken, malice and arrogance everywhere abound to the misery of the people. The sacred places are devastated by the heathen, the altars desecrated by perjury, the monastries defiled by adultery, and the soil of England stained by the blood of its princes. Verily,' concludes Alcuin, 'we are a race of evil-doers, a people laden with iniquity, a sinful nation, whom God will punish as in the olden time, unless we deserve well of Him by earnest prayer, steadfast faith and upright living."[3]

Against the degradation of society which we have just described, the church effected a partial remedy through monasticism. The latter had worked silently for at least a century, before its influence showed itself on the common life of the clergy in the tangible form of a canonical rule. This was one of the chief results of the great ecclesiastical reformation of the Carolingian Age, brought about by the co-operation of church and state.[4] The immediate purpose subserved by the rule was that of discipline; at the same time it made for education and edification, inasmuch as

(1) *Ep.* 124, p. 183. (2) *Ep.* 122, p. 179.
(3) *Epp.* 122, 20, 17, 22.
(4) The first mention of a canonical rule was in the decree of the Council of Vernon in 755—M. G. H. Leg., Sect. II, 1, p. 36. A little later Chrodegang of Metz drew up his famous rule, and in 802 a capitulary of Charles required his priests to live according to the canons under the supervision of a bishop, sleeping in a common dormitory, eating at a common refectory, and living according to a common rule. *Capitulare Missorum Generale,* chaps. 21, 22, M. G. H. Leg., Sect. II, I, pp. 95-96.

the hours of the day and night were apportioned to definite occupations. These, as Alcuin intimates, were chiefly reading and praying.[1] Thus, by means of the canonical rule, the prevalent ignorance of the clergy was lessened, learning became more and more a necessary ingredient of their lives. Furthermore, such great bishops as Arno, Theodulph, Leidrad, and others, arose to lend their whole-souled support to Charles' noble effort to enlighten his people.

(1) *Ep.* 114.

CHAPTER III

DURING the seventh and the early part of the eight centuries, the intellectual life of Frankland had reached a very low ebb. The disorders incident to the Frankish invasion, and the anarchy of the Merovingian rule later on, had forced learning to take refuge in the church and in the monastery. These asylums of learning became so demoralized that those traditions, which had found their way from the ancient Gallic schools into those of the Franks were almost completely lost; of philosophy and literature there was nothing; the Latin language was being forgotten, and when spoken it was without rule or grammar. Worse still, the voice of the teacher was all but silent in the city and in the monastery; idleness and vice had followed hard upon the decline of learning, until monk and priest who ought to have been the intelligent teachers of their people, had degenerated so far as to lose well-nigh even the instinct for moral life,[1]

Conditions would probably have been even worse had not Charles Martel introduced some semblance of order and quiet into society, not alone by his defeat of the Saxons and Saracens, but also by his determined suppression of the Frankish nobles and bishops. By freeing Frankland

(1) Hauréau, B., *Histoire de la Philosophie Scolastique*, part I, p. 3, 6-7; cf. Mullinger, J. B. *Schools of Charles the Great and the Restoration of Education in the Ninth Century*, pp. 37-39: Ebert Ad. *Allgemeine Geschichte der Literatur des Mittelalters in Abendlande*, Vol. II, pp. 3-11.

from dangers without and from dissensions within, by teaching the bishops and abbots that they must do something more than hunt, drink and fight,[1] he prepared the way for Alcuin and Charles, and made possible that intellectual revival which their efforts inaugurated.[2] Nor were evidences of improvement lacking even before their day. Here and there some scholar, like Abbot Gregory of Utrecht, had tried more or less successfully to redeem the character of his school, and to revive learning in his jurisdiction. At Metz, Chrodegang had drawn up his famous rule and inculcated the urgent duty of educating the young. At St. Gall, the monk Winidhar had begun to transcribe manuscripts and so laid the foundations of the noble library there.[3] Thus the Frankish people were ripe for a literary revival; realizing their needs they had become receptive, and already they possessed eager students, both Anglo-Saxon and Frankish, who would give their hearty sympathy and co-operation to him who would promote and organize learning. Such a person was Charles the Great.

It was the aim of Charles to spread secular and ecclesiastical learning among his people, to the end that religion might be promoted, their morals reformed, and their whole intellectual life deepened. Manifestly, his work had to begin with the clergy, for through them, and them alone, as the only teachers of the day[4], could he hope to advance

(1) Cf. *Capitulary of Karlmann,* dated April 21st, 742, cap. 2, M. G. H. Leg.. Sect. II, I, p. 25.

(2) Hauréau, *op. cit.,* part I, pp. 6-7. Cf. Roger, *L'Enseignement des Lettres classiques d'Ausone à Alcuin,* pp. 428-9; Hauck, II, *op. cit.,* pp. 168-71; Gaskoin, *Alcuin,* pp. 171-2; West, *Alcuin,* p. 41.

(3) Hauck, *op. cit.* II, pp. 168-171; Roger, *op. cit.,* pp. 428-429; Gaskoin, *op. cit.,* 173. F. A. Specht, *Geschichte des Unterrichtswesens in Deutschland bis zur Mitte des dreizehnten Jahrhundert,* pp. 10-12, 266-268.

(4) That Charles found much to amend in the lives of his clergy is evident from *capitulary 19,* caps. 15 & 16: "Sacerdotes, qui rite non sapiunt adimplere ministerium suum nec discere iuxta praeceptum . . . . quia ignorantes legem Dei eam aliis annuntiare et praedicare non possunt." M. G. H. Leg. I, p. 46.

the civilization of his people.   Accordingly, he exhorted
the clergy to the study of the Scriptures and of the Liberal
Arts, which they had so long neglected.[1]   "It is our wish,"
says he, "that you may be what it behooves the soldiers
of Christ to be, religious in heart, learned in discourse, pure
in act, so that all that approach your house in order to in-
voke the Divine Master, or to behold the excellence of religious life, may be edified in seeing you and instructed by
hearing your discourse and chant."[2]   Likewise, the whole
people were to devote themselves to learning, laymen were
to send their sons to study 'letters,' and the youths, work-
ing with all diligence, were to remain in school until they
had been instructed in learning.[3]

Fortunately for the furtherance of his educational policy,
Charles could count on the support of such able men as
Alcuin, Paulinus of Aquila, Leidrad of Lyons, and others.
Alcuin set the seal of his enthusiastic approval upon the
plans of Charles for the education of his people.   In a letter
to the latter, he praised him for his zeal in pursuing the
study of the stars, and added: "If only a great many would
imitate your splendid zeal for such studies, mayhap a new
and even more excellent Athens might arise in Frankland,
for this our Athens, having Christ the Lord for its master,
would surpass all the wisdom of the studies of the
Academy."[4]   Evidently Alcuin had high hopes of accomplishing great things for the enlightenment of Frankland.

The tasks which awaited Alcuin and his royal master
were many and varied.   First, the Palace School was to be
reorganized, and the king's own energetic attempts at self-
education superintended; there were the parish, monastic
and cathedral schools to be established or improved, and a

---

(1) "Oblitteratam pene maiorum nostrorum desidia reparare vigil-
ianti studio litterarum." M. G. H. Leg. Sect. II, I, p. 80.
(2) *Ibid.*, Vol. I., p. 79.   (3) *Admonitio Generalis, ibid.*, I, p. 60.
(4) *Ep.* 170.

clergy sufficiently learned and worthy to administer the sacraments was to be created. Finally, it was necessary to
revise the liturgy so as to make it conform to the Roman
use, and it was equally urgent to amend the biblical and
other manuscripts, which were in a most deplorable condition owing to the ignorance of the Merovingian tran-
scribers.

Their task was a gigantic one. The schools were few
in number and woefully defective, while teachers were
very hard to procure.[1] Then, too, books were scarce, inasmuch as many had been lost or destroyed during the
Merovingian period.[2] In one of his letters to Charles,
Alcuin asked permission to send some of his pupils from
Tours to obtain some of the books he had left at York,
in order that the rich fruits of learning might be found
not only in "the gardens there, but also by the pleasant
waters of the Loire."[3] And if the rich abbey of St. Martin's lacked for books,—the abbey supervised by Alcuin himself, and doubtless enriched by his own books, as well as
by copies of those in use at the Palace School,—one can
readily imagine that there must have been scanty if any
traces of a library in the majority of the monasteries elsewhere. Moreover, many of the books were quite untrustworthy, for the manuscripts had been carelessly copied, and
often mutilated, owing to the gross ignorance of the tran-
scribers. Furthermore, the conditions prevailing at that
time increased the difficulties of the mediæval scholar. The
roads were well-nigh impassable; the seas swarmed with

---

(1) "Scholam in eodem coenobio esse instituit quoniam omnes pene
ignaros literarum invenit . . . . optimisque cantilenae sonis, quantum
temporis ordo sinebat, edocuit." *Gesta Abbatum Fontanellensium* a.
787 M. G. H. SS. II, p. 292.
(2) "Sed ex parte desunt mihi, servulo vestro, exquisitiores erudi-
tionis scolasticae libelli, quos habui in patria per bonam et devotissimam
magistri mei industriam vel etiam mei ipsius qualemcumque sudorem."
Ep. 121. Cf. *Ep.* 80.
(3) *Ep.* 121.

pirates, and the land was a prey to chronic warfare.[1] Hence
communication was uncertain and messengers were not to
be relied upon.[2] On more than one occasion Alcuin complained rather bitterly of these untoward circumstances. In
a letter to Sigulfus, he tells us: "Our memory is fickle at
times. We forget what we ought to retain, especially
when we are distracted by worldly affairs, and inasmuch as
we cannot carry our books with us because of their weight,
we must abbreviate at times in order that the precious pearl
of wisdom be light enough for the weary traveller to bear
it with him for his refreshment."[3]

Alcuin gives us elsewhere an even more striking picture
of the difficulties and limitations of scholars in his day. In
his poem *De Sanctis Eboracensis Ecclesiae*, he describes for
us the library of the Cathedral School at York. The latter,
which Alcuin himself had helped to collect, though one of
the largest in its day, seems pitifully small and inadequate
to modern eyes. It is hardly likely that it comprised more
than one or two hundred books; and yet these contain practically all of the learning of that time. It is significant that
Alcuin begins his description of the library by enumerat-
ing the Church Fathers to be found there. At the head
of the list are Jerome, Hilary, Ambrose and Augustine,
after whom come Athanasius, Orosius, Gregory, Leo and
Basil. Fulgentius, Cassiodorus, Chrysostom and John[4] complete the list. Then follow the teachers, philosophers, historians, rhetoricians: these are Aldhelm, Bede, Victorinus,
Boethius, Pompeius and Pliny, together with the 'subtle

(1) *Epp.* 6, 7, 16, 20, 21, 22, 82, 109.
(2) "Sed multum meae nocet devotioni infidelitas accipientium lit-
teras meas vobis dirigendas." *Ep.* 254. Cf. *Epp.* 253, 167, 265, 28.
(3) "Et quia pondera librorum nobiscum portari nequeunt, ideo
aliquoties brevitati studendum est, ut levi sit pondere pretiosa sapientiae
margareta; et habeat fessus ex itinere viator, quo se recreat; licet ex
pondere portantis manus non gravetur." *Ep.* 80.
(4) Probably Jonh of Damascus. Cf. Harnack, V, p. 289.

Aristotle' and the 'mighty rhetorician Tullius.'[1] The classics mentioned by Alcuin are Vergil, Statius and Lucan; they appear at the end of a very considerable list of Christian poets. It is characteristic of Alcuin and of his age that he sees nothing incongruous in associating Vergil with such poets as Sedulius, Juvencus, Alcimus, Clement, Prosper, Paulinus, Arator, Fortunatus and Lactantius. A place of honor is given to the indispensable grammarians, and accordingly the names of Probus, Focas, Donatus, Priscian, Servius, Eutycus, Pompeius, Comminianus, close the list of authors. Neither Isidore of Seville nor Martianus Capella is mentioned, though it is likely that the works of both of these were in the library among the 'many other' books which Alcuin said were to be found there.[2]

In matters of learning and education, Alcuin adopted the same safe and conservative attitude that he had pursued in questions of faith and of religious practice. He and his contemporaries made learning the handmaid of theology; they taught those things only which would be of advantage to religion and to mother church.[3] Their curriculum began and ended with the studies of the Scriptures: scriptural interpretation in its three-fold sense, historical, moral and allegorical, was the keystone of their educational structure.[4] This, Alcuin considered to be the knowledge of most worth;[5] though he by no means despised secular learning.[6]

If the study of the Scriptures is the keystone, the Seven

---

(1) "Acer Aristoteles, rhetor quoquo Tullius ingens." *Versus De Sanct. Eborac. Eccl. op. cit.*, V. 1549.
(2) *Versus De Sanct. Eborac. Eccl. op. cit.*, vv. 1535-1557.
(3) "Quaecunque enim a magistris ad utilitatem sanctarum ecclesiarum Dei didici." *Ep.* 24.
(4) *Vita Alchuini, op. cit.*, cap. 2; *Admonitio Generalis*, cap. 82, M. G. H. Leg. Sect. II, I, p. 161: Rabanus Maurus, *De Clericor. Instit.* III, 2 Migne 107, p. 379. Willibaldi, *Vita S. Bonifatii*, cap. 2: Jaffé, *op. cit.* III, p. 433-35.
(5) *Epp.* 309, 280. (6) *Epp.* 280, 121.

Liberal Arts are the supports of his whole educational system. They are the 'Seven columns which support the dome of wisdom,' the 'seven grades of wisdom' leading up to its summit, which is evangelical perfection.[1] They are the 'seven water-pots,' which have been kept till now to furnish forth the wine that maketh glad the heart of man.[2] As the sole means of arriving at perfect knowledge, the youths ought to study them until 'maturer age and riper judgment' have fitted them for the study of the Scriptures.[3] "On these," says Alcuin, in urging his pupils to study the Liberal Arts, "on these, philosophers have bent their energy; through these, consuls and kings have become illustrious; through these, the venerable Fathers of the church have defended the faith and discomfited the heretic."[4]

However, the Seven Liberal Arts of themselves appear to have had little attraction for the scholars of Alcuin's day; theirs was a relative value, measured by their utility to the church.[5] Latin grammar was studied as the key to the reading and understanding of the Scriptures; metre, rhetoric and dialectic gave the future cleric skill in speech or debate, or in the practical treatment of religious topics; music was of value in connection with the liturgy; arithmetic and astronomy were largely used to determine the date of Easter; while geometry aided the church architect.[6]

Under such circumstances, there could be but little understanding or appreciation of the classical spirit. The

(1) *Ep.* 34. Cf. 280, and Alcuin's *Grammatica*, Migne CI, p. 853.
(2) *Ep.* 309.
(3) *Grammatica*, Migne CI, p. 854.
(4) *Grammatica*, Migne 101, p. 854.
(5) *De Litteris Colendis*, M. G. H. Leg. Sect. II, I, p. 79: *Grammatica*, Migne 101, p. 853: Rabanus Maurus, *De Clericorum*, Instit. book III, cap. 16-Migne CVII, p. 392. Norden, *Die Antike Kunstropsa vom 6ten Jahrhundert vor Christo bis in die Zeit der Renaissance*, Vol. II, p. 680.
(6) Bursian, *Geschichte der Classischen Philologie in Deutschland*, Vol. I, pp. 24-25.

mediæval churchmen regarded the classics merely as an
indispensable aid for the study of the Scriptures.[1] The
early mediæval writers had used the classics wherever they
felt that these would avail Christianity, or serve to embel-
lish their own style.[2] But they had felt impelled to apolo-
gize for those Vergilian phrases which adorned their pages.
They held that amid the noxious superstitions of the ancients there was much which would serve the interests of
truth and of Christianity: they likened themselves to the
Israelites who carried off the gold and silver ornaments of
the Egyptians.[3] This notion of 'despoiling the Egyptians'
still obtained of course in Alcuin's day, and far beyond. In
a letter to Arno, Alcuin admonished him to wash "the
gold" of the classics "free from all dross," so that it might
be purified and rendered acceptable to God and his glorious
Church. Then would the pagan poems, purged from all
filth, be like "a rose bred among thorns, exquisite in frag-
rance, in beauty incomparable."[4] Although Augustine and
others of the fathers had thus assumed an apologetic attitude towards the classics, there had been a growing tendency on the part of some churchmen to regard the study
of the classics as a species of idolatry. Yet, try as they
would, the Christian fathers could not get along without
them at any time during the Middle Ages: the classics
were as necessary to the study of the Liberal Arts as the
latter were for theology. They were particularly essential
for grammar and rhetoric, as Alcuin admitted upon one
occasion when, though roundly denouncing Vergil as a de-

(1) Cassiodorii, *"De Instit. Divin. litter."* c. 28, Migne LXX, pp.
1141-43. *De Litteris Colendis*, M. G. H. Leg. Sect. II, I, p. 79.
(2) Comparetti, *Virgil in the Middle Ages*, p. 65.
(3) Augustine, *De Doctrina Christiana*, II, cap. 40-Migne XXXIV,
p. 63.
(4) "Nam rosa, inter spinas nata miri odoris et coloris incon-
parabilis gratiam habere dinoscitur." *Ep.* 207, p. 345.

ceiver, he conceded that in matters of grammar he was an authority not to be contemned.[1]

As might be expected, the attitude of Alcuin towards the classics was a reflex of that of his predecessors. He exhibited the earlier apologetic but enthusiastic tone of the fathers, together with their later attitude of hostility. Like Augustine, Jerome, and many others, he found the classics necessary. Like them, too, he doubts somewhat the propriety of using them, and is careful at times to explain his grounds for so doing. On the other hand, he is even more outspoken in his opposition to the classics than Tertullian himself. As a boy he had loved the poems of Vergil better than the Psalms.[2] With riper age and experience, however, he adopted a more conservative attitude towards the latter, and professed to despise what he had formerly admired. As he neared the close of his life, he became somewhat narrower in his views and less charitable in spirit. 'That same man,' says his biographer, 'who in his youth had read the lives of Vergil along with the Holy Writ, and the books of the philosophers, in his old age would not allow his monks of Tours to follow the example which he had set at York.'[3] "Are not the divine poets sufficient for you," says Alcuin, "or must you pollute yourselves with the smooth flowing phrases of Vergilian speech?"[4] Certain passages in Alcuin's correspondence also, appear to bear eloquent testimony to a continued acerbity against the classics. Thus he reproached his friend, Ricbodus, Archbishop of Treves, because of his fondness

(1) "Vergilius haud contempnendae auctoritatis falsator," *Ep.* 136. Cf. *Carmen* 32, Poet. Lat. Med. Aev. I, p. 250.
(2) *Vita Alchuini*, cap. 1.
(3) "Legerat isdem vir Domini libros iuvenis antiquorum philosophorum Virgilique mendacia, quae nolebat iam ipse nec audire neque discipulos suos legere," *Vita Alchuini*, cap. 10. Cf. "Haec in Virgiliacis non invenietur mendaciis, sed in euangelica affluenter repperietur veritate." *Ep.* 309, p. 475. Cf. *Ep.* 136. (4) *Vita Alchuini, op. cit.*, cap. 10.

for Vergil. "Lo, a whole year has passed," he writes, "and I have had no letter from you. Ah, if only my name were Vergil, then wouldst thou never forget me, but have my face ever before thee; then should I be 'felix nimium, quo non felicior ullus.' And," he concludes, "would that the four Gospels rather than the twelve Æneids filled your heart."[1]

However, at the very time that he was inveighing most fiercely against the classics in general and Vergil in particular, he was using the latter to illustrate a fact or point a moral. When King Charles sought to inveigle him into coming to the court, in order to debate with some scholars there upon certain astronomical questions, he declined. His refusal is couched in Vergilian phrase. "As the ass is whipped for his sluggishness,[2] so perhaps I, too, have felt not undeservedly the lash of the palace youths. The aged Entellus[3] has long laid aside the cestus and left it for others in the flower of youth. Some of these would strike the old man a mighty blow, so that a mist would come before his eyes and his blood scarce warm again around his heart.[4] Of what avail would the feeble old Flaccus be amid the clash of arms? What can the timid hare do against the wild boars, or the lamb avail against the lions?" "Verily," concludes Alcuin, in declining the king's invitation, "as Vergil wrote to Augustus, so do I to you. 'Tu sectaris apros, ego retia servo.'"[5] Alcuin's letters abound in such references to Vergil.[6] In fact they outnumber three to one the references to all other authors. To be precise, there are twenty-eight references to the classics in the cor-

(1) *Ep.* 13, p. 39.
(2) *Ep.* 145. Cf. Verg. *Georg.* I, 273.
(3) Verg. *Æn.* V, 437 et seq.   (4) Verg. *Georg.* II, 484.
(5) *Ecl.* III, 75, (in *Ep.* 145).
(6) Cf. *Epp.* 178, 215, 145, 175, 164, 162, 13.

respondence of Alcuin. Seven of these are to Horace, Ovid, Terence and Pliny;[1] whereas twenty-one are to Vergil.[2]

Thus, Alcuin, like his predecessors, is inconsistent; he abuses the classics roundly, but uses them upon occasion, and with some effect. The style of Alcuin, like that of most of the literary coterie which gathered at Charles' court, is grammatically correct, and sometimes elegant. To be sure, it lacks spontaneity and tends to mere prettiness of expression, which at times degenerates to bombast. Thus, one of his letters to Theodulph outdoes Lyly's *Euphues* in the wealth of its rhetorical figures and fantastic conceits. He addresses Theodulph as the 'father of the vineyards,' as the custodian of the 'wine-cellars,' wherein has been kept until now the 'good old wine' to be broached in these latter days. "Now by the mercies of God," says he, "a second David is the ruler of a better people, and under him a nobler Zabdi is set over the cellars; for the King hath set his love upon him, and brought him into the wine-cellars,[3] that the scholars may there wreathe him with flowers and comfort him with the flagons[4] of that wine which maketh glad the heart of man."[5] It was passages such as these which led Theodulph and other contemporaries to give Alcuin the palm over all the other writers of the day.[6]

Occasionally we catch glimpses of an imagination trying to soar above the limitations imposed on it by ecclesias-

(1) There are two references to Horace, three to Ovid, one each to Terence and Pliny.

(2) Three references are to the Georgics, seven to the Æneid, eleven to the Eclogues. In regard to Alcuin's attitude towards the classics, cf. O. F. Long, *"Lectures in Honor of Basil L. Gildersleeve,"* pp. 377-86; Comparetti, *"Virgil in the Middle Ages,"* translated by E. F. M. Benecke. (3) *Ep.* 192. (4) *Solomon's Song*, II, 5.

(5) *Psalm* civ, 15. The above translation is taken from West's *"Alcuin,"* p. 79.

(6) "Sit praesto et Flaccus, nostrorum gloria vatum,
Qui potis est lyrico multa boare pede.
Quique sophista potens est, quique poeta melodus
Quique potens sensu, quique potens opere est." *Carmen,* 25, M. G. H. Poet. Lat. Med. Aev. I, p. 486.

tical traditions. Here and there we light upon passages of poetic charm. In carmen 23, for example, he paints a picture which glows for us with something of the beauty and warmth of nature. It may be freely translated thus: "Beloved cell, sweet habitation mine, girt around with whispering trees, and all hidden by the foliage green, before thee stretch the meadows, blooming with fragrant flowers and life-giving herbs; babbling at thy door, the streamlet meanders by, on whose banks, all embowered in flowers, the fisher loves to sit and tend his net. The lily pale, the blushing rose, mingle their odors with the sweet-smelling fruit hanging in rich profusion from thy orchard trees, while, all around, the feathery denizens of the wood swell out their matin song in praise of their Creator."[1] Again, there is something of the spirit of eternal youth in the sprightly lines where he describes himself as "rubbing the sleep of night from his eyes, and leaping from his couch as soon as the ruddy charioteer of dawn suffuses the liquid deep with the new light of day, and then running straightway into the fields of the ancients to pluck their flowers of correct speech and scatter them in sport before his boys."[2] Then, too, there are passages, such as his carmen 25 on Rome, and his farewell epistle to Charles, where something of the dignity of his theme imparts itself to his lines;[3] and his profound grief at the death of his old

(1) "O mea cella, mihi habitatio dulcis, amata. . . .

Undique te cingit ramis resonantibus arbos,
Silvula florigeris semper onusta comis
Prata salutiferis florebunt omnia et herbis,

Flumina te cingunt florentibus undique ripis,
Retia piscator qua sua tendit ovans." *Carmen,* 23, M. G. H. Poet. Lat. Med. Aev. I, p. 243.
(2) "Splendida dum rutilat roseis Aurora quadrigis,
Perfundens pelagus luce nova liquidum," et seq. *Carmen,* 42, M. G. H. Poet. Lat. Med. Aev. I, p. 253, translation by West, p. 47.
(3) *Carmen,* 25, M. G. H. Poet. Lat. Med. Aev. I, p. 245.

master, Elbert, which he so touchingly expresses in his
verses on York, strikes a chord which finds an answering
echo in our own hearts. And certainly much may be for-
given one who could write those beautiful lines of the carmen *In Dormiturio:* "May he who stillest the roaring
winds and raging seas, the God of Israel, who hath never
slept throughout the ages, may He who apportions the day
for work, the night for rest, grant to the weary brethren
sweet refreshing sleep, and dispel with omnipotent hand
the fears which disturb their slumbers."[1]   There is something here of the serenity, the restfulness and the charm
of Goethe's immortal poem "Ein Gleiches."[2]

Alcuin is, however, no stylist and no great scholar. His
forte lay in teaching. He found his opportunity at the
cathedral school at York, the palace school at Aachen, and
the monastic school at Tours, in each of which he taught
the Seven Liberal Arts. Naturally, he paid most attention to grammar, the first and most important, the *sine qua
non* of the other six arts.[3] He himself wrote a *Grammatica,*
based in the main on the earlier grammars of Donatus and
Priscian. The treatise is in the form of a dialogue; first,
there is an explanation by the teacher, which is followed
by questions and answers exchanged between the pupils or
between the master and pupils. The book itself is divided
into two parts; in the first part is discussed the end and
method of education. According to Alcuin, the only thing
worth while is wisdom or 'philosophia,' "the chief adorn-
ment of the soul." "And," says he, "it will not be hard
to point out to you the path of wisdom, if only you will

(1)   *Carmen,* 96, M. G. H. Poet. Lat. Med. Aev. I, p. 321.
(2)   "Ueber allen Gipfelen, ist Ruh," *et seq., in Select Poems of
Goethe,* Ed. of Sonnenschein, p. 6.
(3)   "Haec et origo et fundamentum est artium liberalium," Rabani,
De Clericor. Instit. III, 18, opp. ed., Migne CVII, pp. 395, 396. Cf.
Theodulph, *Carmen,* 46, vv. 1-8, M. G. H. Poet. Lat. Med. Aev. I,
p. 544.

seek after it with the right motive; if, disregarding worldly praise, honor and the deceitful pleasures of wealth, you pursue it for the sake of truth and righteousness. Wisdom is, however, not to be lightly won; there is no royal road; her heights will not be attained until the intervening plains and slopes have been crossed and ascended."[1]

The second portion of the treatise is devoted to grammar. The latter, according to Alcuin, is divided into twenty-six parts,[2] with each of which he proceeds to deal in turn. As an introduction to this there is a discussion of words, letters and syllables, in the form of a dialogue. The latter is carried on between a Saxon and a Frank, in the preface to which dialogue Alcuin states that these, having but recently begun the study of grammatical subtleties, have decided to question each other in order to aid their memory in mastering the rules of grammar. "Do you," says the Frank very significantly, taking the initative, "answer the questions I now propound to you; for you are older than I, being fifteen while I am but fourteen." The Saxon agrees to the proposal, provided that all questions of difficulty be referred to the master. The latter professes himself as well pleased with their proposition, and directs what he calls their 'disputation'[3] by starting them off in a discussion of 'littera.'[4] It runs as follows:

Frank—Why, Saxon, is it called 'littera'?

Saxon—Because the letter prepares the path for the reader.[5]

Frank—Give me then a definition for 'littera.'

Saxon—It is the smallest part of articulate voice.

Both—Master, is there another definition?

(1) *Grammatica,* Migne CI, p. 850.
(2) For an enumeration of these see *Grammatica,* Migne CI, p. 858.
(3) *Ibid.,* p. 854. (4) *Ibid.*
(5) "Littera est quasi legitera, quia legentibus iter praebet," *ibid.,*
p. 855.

Master—There is, but of similar import. The letter is indivisible, because we divide the sentences into parts, and the parts into syllables and the latter into letters, which are thus indivisible.

Both—Why do you call letters, elements?

Master—Because as the members fitly joined together make the body, so the letters make speech.

Frank—State, my fellow pupil, the kinds of letters.

Saxon—They are vowels and consonants, which may be further sub-divided into semi-vowels and mutes. . . .

After they have discussed the vowel and the consonant, they proceed to treat of the syllable in a similar way.

Alcuin next proceeds to treat of the parts of speech. His definitions of these are as faulty as those of the older grammarians upon which they are based. Thus, from his definition[1] of the noun, it appears that he confuses it with the adjective, as the earlier grammarians had done, and while it is true that he feels this confusion, and attempts to give another definition, he fails to make his meaning clear. Evidently, his untrained mind could not distinguish between the object itself and its manifestations or qualities: to him 'sanctus' and 'sanctitas' are both nouns.[2] Moreover, he is not always able to understand and appreciate the differences between his two chief guides, Donatus and Priscian. For example, he is greatly puzzled whether he should follow Donatus and treat of six divisions under the noun, or whether, like Priscian, he should limit himself to five. The chief things which he explains under the noun are its kind, gender, number, case and figures.

The other parts of speech are discussed in a similar way. The verb is treated most extensively; and in the course

(1) "Nomen est pars orationis . . . . quae unicuique corpori vel rei communem vel propriam qualitatem distribuit," *ibid.*, p. 859.

(2) Thus he classes "sanctus" and "sanctitas" among the "denominative" nouns. *Ibid.*, p. 860.

of the dialogue the Saxon gives an appalling list of irregularities in mode and tense.[1] So formidable is it that the Saxon himself is dismayed and discouraged. "Lo, Frank," says he, "what a burden you have laid upon me! What a thorny path you have led me into! Let us have a moment's breathing space, I pray you." "So be it," replies the Frank: "As Vergil saith, 'I shall crush you with this weight.' Yet fear not 'Labor vincit omnia.' "[2] " 'Tis so," agrees the Saxon wearily, "let us continue." And they do, treating of the adverb, participle, conjunction and interjection, which discussion ends the treatise.

Thus Alcuin's conception of grammar is a somewhat different one from that of the grammarians of the late Roman empire. The latter had regarded it as something more than the art of speaking and writing correctly, and had studied literature along with it. Alcuin's grammar, on the other hand, pays no attention to literary form; it is a technical study and by no means a complete one, for it deals almost entirely with etymology.[3] Whatever of value attaches to it may be found in the older grammars of Donatus and Priscian. Yet, imperfect and childish as it is, the *Grammatica* must not be too hastily judged; it may be questioned whether any other kind of grammar would have been as intelligible to the untutored Frank. Its method was simple and attractive; the content, apart from a certain display of erudition, calculated to inspire respect, is not too difficult for the ignorant Frank; on the whole it is well adapted to his need.

Next to the *Grammatica*, Alcuin's most useful educational work is his *Orthography*. This was probably written

(1) *Ibid.*, pp. 878-886. (2) *Ibid.*, p. 885.
(3) This, of course, does not mean that Alcuin paid no attention to syntax or prosody. It is evident he practiced his pupils in the writing of "dictamina." *Ep.* 172. Cf. Monach. Sangall., *De Carolo. M.* I, 3: Jaffé, IV, p. 633.

at Tours, and was designed to help him effect an immediate reform in matters of spelling and copying of the manuscripts. Tours had once been famous for its learning and its copyists; but the writing had degenerated, the manuscripts were full of the grossest errors, and the copyists sorely in need of instruction.[1] They were, also, too much given to trifling and worked too hurriedly. One of his inscriptions in the library, or Scriptorium,[2] warned them against these faults. Elsewhere he admonished his pupils not only to seek out the best possible manuscripts, but also to transcribe them accurately, taking care not to neglect the punctuation. The reader in the Scriptorium was also given wholesome advice "not to read falsely or too rapidly, lest he cause the copyist to make mistakes." Furthermore, in an interesting letter to Charles, Alcuin complained that punctuation, though lending much to the clearness and beauty of sentences, has been neglected owing to the ignorance of the scribes.[3] In fact, the pronunciation and spelling of words had become so unsettled and so confusing as to render some such work as the *Orthography* imperative, if Alcuin and his contemporaries were to leave to their successors reasonably accurate copies of the manuscripts.

In his introduction to the *Orthography*, Alcuin says, "Let him who would reproduce the sayings of the ancients read me; for he who follows me not will speak without regard to law."[4] Then he proceeds to call attention to some of the mistakes in form and spelling made by the barbarian Franks. "Such words," says he, "as *aeternus, actas,* should be spelled with a dipthong '*æ.*'" Another common mistake,

(1) Sulpicius Severus, *Vita S. Martini,* Migne XX, p. 166. Cf. *Admonitio Generalis,* cap. 72, M. G. H. Leg., Sect. II, 60.
(2) *Carmen,* 94, M. G. H. Poet. Lat. Med. Aev. I, p. 320.
(3) *Ep.* 172, p. 285.
(4) "Me legat antiquas vult qui proferre loquelas, Me qui non sequitur, vult sine lege loqui," Migne CI, p. 902.

according to Alcuin, was the confusion of '*b*', not alone with '*v*,' but even with '*f*' and '*u*.' "Thus," says Alcuin, "if you mean *wool*, write *vellus;* if *beautiful*, write *bellus*."[1] The misuse of the aspirate is another subject of which Alcuin treats. "*Habeo* should be written with an '*h*' and aspirated, whereas the reverse is true of *abeo*. Nor must it be forgotten," he adds, "that '*h*' aspirate may be used before all vowels, but after four consonants only, namely, *c, t, p, r*."[2] The doubling of such consonants as *l, m, n*,[3] as well as the interchange of the last two, in prefixes, comes in for some consideration. Alcuin, moreover, is aware of what the modern grammarians call the principle of ease; for example, he points out that the frequent change of *b* into *f* or *g* in prefixes, as in the case of *suffero* and *suggero,* is due to a desire to secure ease of pronunciation.[4] By far the most diverting features of the *Orthography* are those portions where he intersperses his treatment of rules, irregularities and mistakes by some very peculiar examples of 'derivations,' as, for instance, "'*Coelebs*,' *qui sibi iter facit ad coelum*."[5] From the standpoint of philology, the *Orthography* is quite important as illustrating a transitional stage of the Latin language. The latter, which had already conquered the Celtic language, is here seen to be confronted with the Germanic, and their reaction upon each other resulted in great confusion.

Alcuin's remaining works on the *Trivium*, the *De Rhe-*

---

(1) Migne CI, pp. 902-903. Cf. Isidore, *Etymologiarum,* Book I, cap. 27. Migne, Vol. LXXXII, p. 101.

(2) "*H* aspiratio ante vocales omnes poni potest; post consonantes autem quatuor tantumodo, *c, t, p, r,*" Migne CI, p. 910. Cf. Isidore, *op. cit.,* Migne LXXXII, p. 102.

(3) "*Malo,* id est magis volo; et nolo, id est ne volo per unum l. Malle, velle et nolle per due l." *Ibid.,* CI, p. 911. Cf. Isidore, *op. cit.,* LXXXII, pp. 102-3.

(4) "Saepe *b* in praepositione sub euphoniae causa im sequentem mutabitur consonantem ut *suffero, suggero,*" Migne CI, p. 916. Cf. Isidore, *op. cit.,* cap. 27, pp. 101-102.

(5) Migne, CI, p. 906.

torica et Virtutibus and the *Dialectica* are less important. They bear testimony to Alcuin's weakness in the field of rhetoric and dialectic. They are based on the works of his predecessors, and not the least remarkable thing about them is the uncontrovertible evidence they afford that Alcuin allowed himself to copy whole sentences and even paragraphs *ad libitum* from the works of Isidore of Seville and the Fathers. It is plain that he fears to disagree with these; he considers himself happy, if, peradventure, he understand the thoughts of the ancients through their interpretation. Thus in his introduction to the *Dialectica,* he says: "He who reads this book will praise the wonderful genius of the ancients, and will strive so far as in him lieth to attain unto like wisdom."[1] The first of these works, the *De Rhetorica et Virtutibus,* is based on the writings of Cicero and of Isidore, whose ideas Alcuin reproduces with great loss to their originals as far as form and force are concerned. For the rules, principles, and main divisions of his rhetoric, he draws largely upon Cicero's *De Inventione,* which he quotes at times word for word.[2] His second source is Isidore, whom he cites quite as freely. Hence, we find in the *Rhetorica* the five divisions, the three kinds of rhetorical speech, the six parts of an oration, which meet us in Cicero's *De Inventione* and Isidore's *Etymologies.*[3] There is, however, one part of the treatise where he is more

---

(1) *De Dialectica,* Migne CI, p. 951. Cf. *Carmen,* 77, M. G. H. Poet. Lat. Med. Aev. I, p. 298.

(2) Thus Alcuin borrows Cicero's well-known passage, "Nam Fuit quoddam tempus, cum in agris homines passim bestiarum modo vagabantur." Cf. *Opera Rhetorica,* Ed. G. Friederich, Vol. I, pt. I, p. 118.

(3) "Artis Rhetoricae partes quinque sunt; inventio, dispositio, elocutio, memoria, et pronuntiatio," Migne CI, p. 921. Cf. Isidore, *Etymologiarum.*" Book 2, cap. 3, Vol. LXXXII, p. 125. "Ars quidem rhetoricae in tribus versatur generibus id est demonstrativo, deliberativo, judiciali," Rhetorica Migne CI, p. 922. Cf. Isidore, *op. cit.,* cap. 4, p. 125. "Sex sunt partes, per quas ab oratore ordinanda est oratio. Causae exordium, narratio, confirmatio, partitio, reprehensio, conclusio," Migne CI, p. 929. Isidore has but four of these.

original. This is the portion that deals with the application of rhetoric to suits at law. In the dialogue between Charles and Alcuin which serves as an introduction to this work, he defines rhetoric as the art of "good speaking," but he goes on to explain that it also treats of civil questions.[1] "Just as," says he, "it is natural for us to attack an enemy and to defend ourselves, so we are prone to justify ourselves and blame others, but he who has perfected himself in the art of rhetoric will protect himself more skilfully; he will excel all others in debate, even as the skilled soldier will overcome him who has no training in the use of arms." It was this practical side of rhetoric which appealed to Charles. "Teach me the rules of rhetoric, I pray thee," the latter says, "for every day I have need of them."[2] Accordingly, Alcuin proceeds to define rhetoric, to state its divisions and to show how it may be applied in conducting and determining civil suits. Herein lies its chief significance: it is one of those works that serves to mark the transition from the earlier technical treatment of the subject in ancient times to the later and more practical treatment in the Middle Ages as seen in the text-books of the *Dictamen.* Such a work as Alcuin's *Rhetorica* goes far to bear out Rashdall's contention that it was customary in the Middle Ages to study rhetoric as an aid in the composition of legal documents.[3]

But the most characteristic thing about Alcuin's *Rhetorica* is the persistence with which the moral aspects of the subject are emphasized. This is apparent even in the earlier and more technical part of the treatise. Thus, there is a tendency to explain rhetorical principles by illus-

(1) "In civilibus quaestionibus, quae naturali animi ingenio concipi possint," *ibid.*, p. 921. Cf. Isidore, *op. cit.*, p. 140, where the same phrase occurs word for word. Cf. *Carmen*, 82, M. G. H. Poet. Lat. Med. Aev. I, p. 300.
(2) Migne CI, p. 921.
(3) H. Rashdall, *Universities in the Middle Ages*, Vol. I, p. 94.

trations from the scriptures.[1] Again, when Charles asks Alcuin how he may strengthen the memory, the latter enjoins him to avoid intemperance, the chief foe of all liberal studies, the destroyer of bodily health, and of mental soundness.[2] Here Alcuin implies that rhetoric will avail the orator but little unless he be virtuous : if he have not a proper knowledge of the human heart, its joys, its sorrows and its virtues, his words will have no power. It is this conviction, probably, which led Alcuin to close his treatise with a short description of the four cardinal virtues, prudence, justice, fortitude and temperance. In the introduction to this part of the treatise, he says : "There are certain things so splendid and so noble that the mere possession of them is a sufficient reward in itself; one honors and loves them for a dignity which is all their own." Charles, much impressed, asks what these may be. "They are virtue, knowledge, truth, pure love," rejoins Alcuin, "and they are honored by Christians and philosophers alike." [3] A discussion of the above mentioned cardinal virtues and their various subdivisions ends the treatise.

Closely associated with rhetoric in Alcuin's day was the study of dialectic. In his *Dialectica,* he explains their relation to each other. "They differ," says he, "as the clenched fist from the open hand; the one masses its arguments with directness and precision, while the other develops them through discoursive eloquence.'[4] As is well known, the *Dialectica* is based on the pseudo-Augustinian work on the categories and on Isidore's *Etymologies.*[5] Alcuin does not

(1) Notably his citation of Paul's defense before Felix, as an instance of the use of the *deliberativum,* Migne CI, p. 922. (2) *Ibid.,* p. 941. (3) *Ibid.,* pp. 943-4.
(4) "Dialectica et rhetorica est, quod in manu hominis pugnus astrictus et palma distenta," et seq. *ibid.,* p. 953. Cf. Isidore, *op. cit.,* Book 2, cap. 23, where the same idea is found in almost identical words.
(5) Categoriae decum—Migne, Vol. XXXII, pp. 1419-1440, cf. Prantl, C., *Geschichte der Logik im Abendlande,* II, p. 14. *Etymologiarum, op. cit.,* infra, Book 2.

dream of excelling these authorities, but very complacently
sets to work to reproduce them. The result is one of the
most consistent pieces of plagiarism that has ever been
produced. There is scarcely an original idea throughout
the whole *Dialectica;* its plan, subject divisions, chapter
headings, and nomenclature, are the same as in the above
mentioned works; whole sentences, nay, whole paragraphs
are copied, in some places word for word. Thus in his
introductory chapter, he divides philosophy into physics,
ethics and logic, and these are further subdivided; physics
into arithmetic, geometry, music and astronomy; ethics
into the four cardinal virtues, prudence, justice, fortitude
and temperance; logic, into rhetoric and dialectic. Under
the latter he treats of isagogues, categories, syllogisms,
definitions, topics, and the perihermenies. These divisions,
together with their explanations and definitions, are almost
identical with those we find in Isidore's work.[1] The same
is true of the second chapter, which deals with the isagogues. The second division of the treatise, comprising
chapters three to ten inclusive, is based on a similar work
long ascribed to Augustine.[2] Here Alcuin follows his
source even more closely than in the first two chapters:
not only are the ten Aristotelian categories the same as

(1) The following passages show the extent to which Alcuin has
copied from Isidore. Alcuin's introduction reads: "Philosophia est
naturarum inquisitio, rerum humanarum; divinarumque cognitio; quantum homini possibile est aestimare," Migne CI, cap. 1, p. 952. Cf.
Isidore: "Philosophia est rerum humanarum divinarumque cognitio cum
studio bene vivendi conjuncta. Item aliqui doctorum; Philosophia est
divinarum humanarumque rerum in quantum homini possibile est,"
Isidore, *op. cit.,* Book 2, cap 24, Vol. LXXXII, pp. 140-141. "In quot
partes dividitur philosophia? In tres; physiciam, ethicam, logicam.
Haec quoque latino ore exprome. Physica est naturalis, ethica moralis,
logica rationalis," *Dialectica,* p. 952. Cf. "Philosophiae species tripartita
est una naturalis, quae Graece physica appellatur, altera moralis quae
Graece ethica dicitur; tertia rationalis quae Graeco vocabulo logica
appellatur," *Etymologiarum, op. cit.,* p. 141.
(2) Alcuin believed Augustine was the author, as is evident from
his citation in cap. 10 of *Dialectica:* "Augustinus magnus orator filius
illius."

those found in the pseudo-Augustinian work, but they are discussed in just the same way and at times in identical language.[1] Nor is Alcuin any more original in the last part of the treatise, where he once more reverts to Isidore as his source in his discussion of the "topics" and the "periher-menies."[2] Thus, Alcuin's proud boast made in the introduction to the effect that "he had brought treasurers of wisdom from over the sea"[3] was not without foundation. These treasures were not his own, however, nor, to do him justice, would he have claimed that they were. In conclusion we may say that a study of the *Rhetorica* and the *Dialectica* goes far to prove that while the reign of rhetoric was over in Alcuin's day, the mediæval *régime* of dialectics had not yet begun. Nevertheless, inferior as Alcuin's treatises on these subjects were, it would seem that the *Dialectica* must have played a great part in promoting the study of logic in Europe, by reason of the number of his pupils and the influence he exerted over them.[4]

The quadrivium, (or mathematical subjects), consisted of arithmetic, geometry, music and astronomy. In comparison with these, the trivium was considered child's play.[5] While secular education was by no means restricted to the study of the latter, there can be no doubt but that the quadrivium was much more essential to the clergy than to the laity. Arithmetic and astronomy were particularly indispensable for computing the correct date of Easter.[6]

(1) For a comparison of citations from the two works, see Monnier's *Alcuin*, p. 48. (2) The "topics" is based on Isidore, cap 30, Migne, Vol. LXXXII, pp. 151-153; that on the "perihermenies" is based on cap. 27, Migne, LXXXII, p. 145.

(3) *Dialectica*, Migne CI, p. 951. Cf. *Carmen*, 77, M. G. H. Poet. Lat. Med. Aev. I, p. 298.

(4) Cf. P. Abelson, *Seven Liberal Arts*, p. 80, note I.

(5) Bonifatii, *Ep.* 3. Jaffé, *op. cit.* III, p. 33.

(6) Charles insisted on his clergy's knowing how to calculate the dates of church holidays and to arrange the calendar for the year. Cf. *Admonitio Generalis*, C, 72, M. G. H. Leg. Sect. II, I, 60. Cf. "Quae a presbyteris discenda sint," c. 8, *Ibid.* I, p. 110.

Alcuin bore witness to this and at the same time complained
that mathematics were almost entirely neglected in his day.[1]
However, thanks to the personal interest and earnest efforts
of Charles, much progress was made in these subjects.[2]

Alcuin himself wrote little on the quadrivium. So far
as arithmetic is concerned, it is just possible that he regarded it as so indispensable a part of education, that he did
not think it worth while to write upon it, unless to explain
some of its special or difficult phases.[3] It is certain from
Alcuin's description of the school at York that he knew
enough of arithmetic to teach the subject.[4] It does not
seem likely that he went beyond the simple operations of
addition, subtraction and multiplication.[5] These were con-
ducted by means of finger reckoning and the reckoning
board,[6] on which *nummi* or *calculi* were used.[7] It does
not seem very probable that he knew the *abacus* or the
apices, inasmuch as these did not come into general use
until after Alcuin's day.[8]

The only arithmetical work ascribed to Alcuin is his possibly spurious *Propositiones ad acuendos juvenes.* These

(1) "Obprobrium est grande, ut dimittamus eas perire diebus nos-
tris." *Ep.* 148, p. 239.
(2) Charles brought "computists" from Italy. *Nota ad annales
Lauriss,* a. 787, M. G. H. SS. I, 171. Compare *Ep.* 126, 145, Einhart, *Vita
Caroli,* c. 25, M. G. H. SS. II.
(3) Cantor, M., *Mathematische Beiträge zum Kulturleben der Völker,"* p. 286.
(4) *Versus de Sanctus Eborac. Eccles.* v, 1445, *et seq.*
(5) Cantor, M., *Vorlesungen über Geschichte der Mathematik,* Vol.
I, p. 839. Ball, W. R. R., *A Short Account of the History of Mathematics,* p. 125.
(6) Friedlein, G., *Die Zahlzeichen und das Elementare Rechnen der
Griechen und Römer und des Christlichen Abendlandes, vom 7ten bis
13ten Jahrhundert,* p. 50. Hankel, H., *Zur Geschichte der Mathematik
im Altertum und Mittelalter,* p. 309. *Computus vel loquela digitorum,*
Bede, Migne, Vol. XC, p. 295.
(7) *Ep.* 149, p. 243.
(8) Hankel, *op. cit.,* p. 317. J. Cajori, *A History of Elementary
Mathematics,* p. 112. Cantor, however, thinks that Alcuin may have
had some knowledge of the "apices." He bases his opinion upon two
references (*Ep.* 133 and *Versus de Sanctus Eborac. Eccles.,* v 1445).
Cf. Cantor, *op. cit.,* p. 839.

are problems or rather riddles, designed to entertain or please the reader.[1] Some of them are soluble by algebraical and geometrical means; others are insoluble save by an exercise of wit and of dialectics. To the latter class belongs the problem of the wolf, the goat, and the cabbage-head.[2] In some of the problems, Alcuin is the immediate imitator of the Romans, the indirect imitator of the Greeks.[3] Thus the famous problem of the hound and the hare, and the equally noted one of the will, as well as many others, came down to him from the Greeks and the Romans.[4] A slight study of the problems shows us that even if Alcuin be their author, the mathematicians of his day knew little more than addition, subtraction, multiplication and division. They appear to have had some knowledge of square root and of fractions, but they knew no geometry, save a few useful formulæ for practical purposes in measurement, while in algebra they did not go beyond simple equations.

Alcuin put arithmetic to a use other than of the ordinary one of computing Easter. After the example of Augustine, Cassiodorus, and Gregory the Great, he applied the theory of numbers to the explanation of Scripture. He knew how to find a significance in every number used in the Bible, and he strongly recommends that all clerics be educated in the "science of numbers."[5] In his treatment of numbers, he classifies them as perfect and imperfect. Thus, six is a perfect number because it is equal to the sum of its divisors, one, two, three, whereas eight is a defective number, being greater than the sum of its divisors, one,

(1) Cajori, *op. cit.,* p. 113. Cantor, *op. cit.,* p. 835. Hagen, H., *Antike und Mittelälterliche Rätselpoesie,* 2nd Edn., pp. 29-34.
(2) Problem 18, Migne CI, p. 1149.
(3) Cantor, M., *Die Römischen Agrimensoren und ihre Stellung in der Geschichte der Feldmesserkunst,* pp. 143-144.
(4) Cf. Problems 19 and 26, *ibid.,* pp. 1150, 1155.
(5) *Alcuini Exposit. in psalm. Ponit. praef. ad Arnonem,* Migne C, p. 573.

ing its sessions wherever the King had his court, fulfilled
a noble purpose in fitting such young men for their life
work, through the agency of the greatest teacher of his
time.   There can be little doubt but that Charles' well-
known penchant for well educated servants in church and
state, brought many aspirants for his favor to the Palace
School.   Consequently, as he was aiming to produce states-
men as well as churchmen, he desired Alcuin to instruct
the pupils of the school in something more than the chant,
the reading of Latin, and the calculating of Easter.   Furthermore, the latter not only did impart to his pupils the
practical knowledge that fitted them for preferment in
church and state, but, as he himself proudly states,[1] he
also gave them instruction in all those branches of knowledge that had come down from the Romans.

The Palace School was composed of the royal family,
the young nobles and officials of the King, together with all
those who sought position and preferment,[2] the only
avenue to which lay in compliance with Charles' wish that
they should first fit themselves for it by education.[3]   Gundrada, together with other ladies of the royal family, were
present, lending grace and brightness to that charmed
circle, the Round Table of the Franks, as it might be called.
And of course, the Round Table would not be complete
without its Arthur, the mighty Charles, whom Alcuin
sometimes designates as Solomon, because of his wisdom,
though more frequently he calls him David on account of
his warlike prowess.[4]   To the members of this circle, their
teacher gave new names, partly in accordance with custom, partly as a reminder that they were going to begin a

(1)   *Alcuini de Studiis in aula regia, Carmen*, 26, M. G. H. Poet. Lat.
Med. Aev., I, pp. 245, 246.   (2)   Einhard, *Vita*, cap. 19.
(3)   *Capitularies* 22, 38, 43, 116, 117, also *Monach. Sangall.*   Book
I, cap. 3, M. G. H. SS. II, p. 732.
(4)   *Epp.* 229, 231, 143.

and is said to have written a book on music which has disappeared. Throughout his period, music was more of a speculative science than an art.

As a teacher, Alcuin had ample opportunity to carry on his great work under circumstances which were calculated to make him the most potent educational force of his day. York was the educational centre of England, Tours was one of the oldest and greatest monasteries of France, while the Palace School was the capstone of Charles' educational system. It was Alcuin's good fortune to teach in all of these places. The system of education planned by Charles, and partially carried out by his bishops and archbishops, made provision for elementary and secondary instruction in a parish school,[1] presided over by the parish priest. Next came the monastic or cathedral schools, which likewise furnished elementary instruction; though in some cases, they also gave instruction in the higher branches of learning. Over them was the abbot or scholasticus appointed by the bishop. At the head of the system, intended in a measure as a model for the lower schools, stood the Palace School.[2].

The origin of this school which thus occupied an unique position in the system of Charlemagne has long been a debated question.[3] It would be idle for us to enter into a discussion of it here. Suffice it to say that it seems safe to conclude, that the Great King gathered around him the noble youths of his kingdom—youths destined for high preferment in church or state, and that these youths constituted the Palace School; that furthermore, the school hold-

---

(1) *Admonitio Generalis,* a. 789, c. 72. M. G. H. Leg. Sect. II, **1,** p. 60.
(2) *Epistola Litteris Colendis, ibid.,* I, p. 79.
(3) For the origin of the Palace School see the following: Mullinger, p. 68, footnote 3; Hauck, II, p. 121; Monnier, pp. 56-59; Lorenz, p. 23; Werner, p. 22; Denk, *Gallo-Frankisches Unterrichts und Bildungswesen,* p. 246; Specht, *Geschichte des Unterrichtswesen in Deutschland,* pp. 3-5, 18, together with authorities there cited.

graphical, cosmological encyclopedia.[1] It was a comprehensive text-book, giving instruction in such things as chronology, the course of the sun, moon and stars, the changes of the season, meteorology, climate, and geography. And we have it on record that Alcuin himself studied these things at York.[2] Moreover, he knew enough about astronomy to go beyond Bede to Pliny's *Natural History,* whose second book he asked Charles to send him.[3]

The remaining members of the quadrivium, music and geometry, may be dismissed with a word. The latter was practically neglected until the eleventh century.[4] It dealt, not so much with geometry as we understand the term, as with mensuration, geography and kindred subjects. Thus it taught how to find the area of triangles, rectangles and circles by the same formula of approximation which the Egyptians and Boethius had used.[5] And it would seem that it taught something of the size and form of the earth, of the disposition of land and water, of zones, tides, and eclipses, together with some natural history.[6] As for music, it was indispensable for the services of the church, and as such, was one of the most important of the quadrivium. Charles did much to promote it in the monastic and cathedral schools by bringing singers from Rome, and by establishing special schools to teach the chant.[7] Alcuin paid special attention to the teaching of singing at Tours,

---

(1) Werner, *Bede der Ehrwurdige,* p. 93. Cf. *Monumenta Germania Paedogogica,* Vol. III, p. 5. Wattenbach, *Geschichtsquellen,* p. 130.
(2) *Versus de Sanct. Eborac., Eccles., op. cit.,* vv, 1430-1445. *Ep.* 155, p. 250.
(3) *Ep.* 155, p. 250.
(4) Specht, *Unterrichtswesens in Deutschland,* p. 144.
(5) *Alcuini propositiones ad accuendos juvenes.* Migne, CI, pp. 1143-60.
(6) *Versus de Sanct. Eborac., Eccles,* op. cit., vv. 1439-1445.
(7) *Additam. Engolism. ad. ann. Lauriss. maj.* a. 788, M. G. H. SS. I, pp. 170, 171. Cf. *Chronic. Moissiac. ad. a.* 802, M. G. H. SS. I, p. 306.

and is said to have written a book on music which has
disappeared. Throughout his period, music was more of a
speculative science than an art.

As a teacher, Alcuin had ample opportunity to carry on
his great work under circumstances which were calculated
to make him the most potent educational force of his day.
York was the educational centre of England, Tours was
one of the oldest and greatest monasteries of France, while
the Palace School was the capstone of Charles' educational
system. It was Alcuin's good fortune to teach in all of
these places. The system of education planned by Charles,
and partially carried out by his bishops and archbishops,
made provision for elementary and secondary instruction in
a parish school,[1] presided over by the parish priest. Next
came the monastic or cathedral schools, which likewise furnished elementary instruction; though in some cases, they
also gave instruction in the higher branches of learning.
Over them was the abbot or scholasticus appointed by the
bishop. At the head of the system, intended in a measure
as a model for the lower schools, stood the Palace School.[2].

The origin of this school which thus occupied an unique
position in the system of Charlemagne has long been a
debated question.[3] It would be idle for us to enter into
a discussion of it here. Suffice it to say that it seems safe
to conclude, that the Great King gathered around him the
noble youths of his kingdom—youths destined for high preferment in church or state, and that these youths constituted the Palace School; that furthermore, the school hold-

(1) *Admonitio Generalis,* a. 789, c. 72. M. G. H. Leg. Sect. II, 1,
p. 60.
(2) *Epistola Litteris Colendis, ibid.,* I, p. 79.
(3) For the origin of the Palace School see the following: Mullinger, p. 68, footnote 3; Hauck, II, p. 121; Monnier, pp. 56-59; Lorenz,
p. 23; Werner, p. 22; Denk, *Gallo-Frankisches Unterrichts und Bildungswesen,* p. 246; Specht, *Geschichte des Unterrichtswesen in
Deutschland,* pp. 3-5, 18, together with authorities there cited.

graphical, cosmological encyclopedia.[1] It was a comprehensive text-book, giving instruction in such things as chronology, the course of the sun, moon and stars, the changes of the season, meteorology, climate, and geography. And we have it on record that Alcuin himself studied these things at York.[2] Moreover, he knew enough about astronomy to go beyond Bede to Pliny's *Natural History,* whose second book he asked Charles to send him.[3]

The remaining members of the quadrivium, music and geometry, may be dismissed with a word. The latter was practically neglected until the eleventh century.[4] It dealt, not so much with geometry as we understand the term, as with mensuration, geography and kindred subjects. Thus it taught how to find the area of triangles, rectangles and circles by the same formula of approximation which the Egyptians and Boethius had used.[5] And it would seem that it taught something of the size and form of the earth, of the disposition of land and water, of zones, tides, and eclipses, together with some natural history.[6] As for music, it was indispensable for the services of the church, and as such, was one of the most important of the quadrivium. Charles did much to promote it in the monastic and cathedral schools by bringing singers from Rome, and by establishing special schools to teach the chant.[7] Alcuin paid special attention to the teaching of singing at Tours,

---

(1) Werner, *Bede der Ehrwurdige,* p. 93. Cf. *Monumenta Germania Paedogogica,* Vol. III, p. 5. Wattenbach, *Geschichtsquellen,* p. 130.

(2) *Versus de Sanct. Eborac., Eccles., op. cit.,* vv, 1430-1445. *Ep.* 155, p. 250.

(3) *Ep.* 155, p. 250.

(4) Specht, *Unterrichtswesens in Deutschland,* p. 144.

(5) *Alcuini propositiones ad accuendos juvenes.* Migne, CI, pp. 1143-60.

(6) *Versus de Sanct. Eborac., Eccles, op. cit.,* vv. 1430-1445.

(7) *Additam. Engolism. ad. ann. Lauriss. maj.* a. 788, M. G. H. SS. I, pp. 170, 171. Cf. *Chronic. Moissiac. ad.* a. 802, M. G. H. SS. I, p. 306.

two, four, and he goes on to explain that the number of beings created by God is six, because six is a perfect number, and God created all things well. Seven, likewise, being composed of one and six is a perfect number. And he adds that God completed the creation in six days to show that he had done all things well.[1] An even better example of his science of numbers is in Epistle 260, where he deals with the numbers from one to ten, and explains their significance. "As there is one ark," says Alcuin, "in which the faithful were saved amid a perishing world, so there is one Holy Church wherein the faithful may be saved, though the sinners perish; and as there was one flight of the children of Israel through the Dead Sea to the promised land, so there is one baptism, through which alone one may attain to eternal life."[2]

A knowledge of astronomy was quite as important as arithmetic in computing the date of Easter. King Charles did much to promote the study of this subject; his letters to Alcuin not only attest his desire to have a correct calendar,[3] but they also evince a genuine liking for the subject itself. Astronomy, in fact, became a sort of fad; the ladies of the court took it up.[4] Alcuin's book, the *De cursu et saltu lunæ ac bissexto,* dealt merely with the astronomy of the computus; but it is quite evident that he knew a great deal more of the subject than the mere technical skill required in calculating Easter. To begin with, Alcuin was familiar with Bede's Book *De Natura Rerum,* that cosmo-

---

(1) Likewise three and four are also perfect numbers, the first because it represents the Trinity, the second because it stands for the four parts of the world, or the four cardinal virtues, or the four Gospels. Cf. *Comemntary on Apocalypse,* Migne C, p. 1130. *Commentary on Genesis, ibid.,* pp. 520-521. Cf. *Ep.* 81.

(2) *Ibid.* Cf. Cajori, *op. cit.,* p. 113.

(3) *Epp.* 145, 456, 155, 170. Einhard, *Vita Caroli, op. cit.,* cap. 25, M. G. H. SS. Vol. II, p. 456. (4) "Noctibus inspiciat caeli mea filia stellas." *Carmen,* 26, v. 41, M. G. H. Poet. Lat. Med. Aev., I, p. 246.

new life, entirely different from that warlike and barbarous one in which they had been nurtured.[1]

With such a coterie of friends and pupils, ranging in age from mere youths to men experienced in council and war, Alcuin had no easy task. It must have been particularly difficult to interest and instruct such a heterogeneous circle to the benefit of all. And yet, for fourteen long years he ministered to the needs of his different pupils with unwavering enthusiasm and tireless energy. While he instilled the rudiments of knowledge into the minds of the youth, he also found time to direct the studies and solve the difficulties of the older members of the circle. They studied the Seven Liberal Arts, paying special attention to the studies of grammar and rhetoric, seeking to perfect themselves in elegance of expression by a careful study of the masterpieces of the ancients.[2] At times, however, he grew weary and a little restive, under the constant questioning, the not infrequent baiting to which he was subjected. Thus, questioned by one, cross-questioned by another, the old man sometimes doubled in his tracks, and made mistakes. This he admitted long afterwards when at Tours. "The horse," he quaintly remarks, "which has four legs often stumbles, how much more must man who has but one tongue often trip in speech." To such vexatious experiences were superadded the tiring journeys of the court and the interruption of his studies due to his abbatial duties, all of which made the old scholar often long for the peaceful seclusion of the cloister. This, in a measure, he was to obtain as Abbot of Tours, whither Charles sent him to reform the monks and possibly, also,

---

(1) "Saepe familiaritas nominis inmutationem solet facere; sicut ipse Dominus Simonem mutavit in Petrum, et filios Zebedei filios nominavit tonitrui," *Ep.* 241.
(2) *Ep.* 172.

to establish a school which would serve as a model for the other monasteries in Frankland.[1]

Alcuin assumed the task with great zeal. The monastic school at Tours as well as those elsewhere had greatly declined. Since these were the main outfitters for the parish priest, Alcuin felt that it was high time for reform. He regarded the monastic and cathedral schools as necessary to perpetuate a priesthood which would be able to defend the doctrines of the Catholic Church and defend her ritual. And the troublous condition of the times, together with the fate of learning in his own country of Northumbria, may well have made him anxious as to the outlook in Frankland. His letter to the Archbishop of Canterbury admonishing him "to promote learning among the household of God, teaching the youths to study the books, and to learn the chant so that the dignity of the church may be upheld,"[2] probably represents the position which he would have the monastic and cathedral schools in Frankland occupy.

The instruction imparted in Alcuin's school at Tours was necessarily more in accordance with the traditions of the church than that which he had dispensed as Master of the Palace School. True, he pursued the same studies, but in a narrower spirit, taking as his model his old school at York. He himself describes what he taught at Tours, and how he directed his pupils. "In accordance with your exhortation and desire," he writes to Charles, "I, your Flaccus, strive to minister unto some of the Brotherhood at St. Martins, the honeys of Holy Scriptures; others, I seek to inebriate with the old wine of the ancient Scriptures; others, I am beginning to nourish on the 'apples of grammatical sub-

(1) "Equus, quattuor habens pedes, saepe cadit; quanto magis homo, unam habens linguam, per vices cadit in verbo?" *Ep.* 149. Cf. *Carmen*, 42, M. G. H. Poet. Lat. Med. Aev., *op. cit.*, I, pp. 253, 254.
(2) *Ep.* 128, p. 190. Cf. *Epp.* 31, 226.

tlety;' others, again, I try to initiate into the mysteries of the stars."[1] He taught the Liberal Arts at Tours as he had taught them at York and at the Palace School. Naturally, however, a school whose chief purpose was to prepare priests for the church would emphasize the teaching of grammar, the study of the Scriptures and the Fathers, the learning of the chant, and the art of copying and illuminating the manuscripts.[2] That was the program for the majority of the pupils; a few of the older and more mature, however, studied in addition astronomy, the "science of numbers" together with philosophy, or as Alcuin terms it, "the acute disquisitions of the wise men on the nature of things."[3] Some of the most advanced pupils who enjoyed his confidence and affection were made companions in labor, collecting and verifying patristic citations for his controversial works.[4]

Alcuin was very much at home in Tours. He was engaged in the vocation of teaching for which he was best fitted. He worked along traditional lines after the model of the cathedral school at York. We cannot conceive of his tolerating at Tours those irregularities, digressions, informal discussions and excursions into all sorts of unbeaten paths which had vexed his patient soul while teaching in the Palace School. We may be sure that he followed in his own classes that advice which he had given to his friend Eanbald of York: "Provide masters both for the boys and the clerks," says he, "arrange into separate classes those who practice the chant, those who study the books, and those who do the copying."[5] Such a division gave each one the work for which he was best fitted, while it also made for discipline.

(1) *Ep.* 121, pp. 176-177, translation by West, p. 66.
(2) *Carmen,* 93. *Die Scola et Scholasticis,* M. G. H. Poet. Lat. Med. Aev., *op. cit.,* I, pp. 319-320. Cf. *Ep.* 121.
(3) Gaskoin, *op. cit.,* p. 193.   (4) *Ep.* 149, p. 244.   (5) *Ep.* 114.

Alcuin would tolerate neither idleness nor levity. In that same letter to Eanbald he wrote: "Let each class have its own master, so that the boys be not allowed to run about in idleness, nor engage in silly play."[1] The pupils, moreover, were to be punctual; the "Admonitio juvenum" urged the boys to open their eyes immediately when the bell rang for matins.[2] Another inscription over the door of the school recommended the students to be diligent, and the masters to be indulgent.[3] Thus was justice tempered with mercy. Alcuin, himself, though he knew how to be firm, was very sympathetic and at times playful in his attitude towards his pupils. His inscription over the dormitories wishing his boys sweet repose in the name of One who never slept is a veritable benediction.[4]

In other respects Alcuin was a modern, nay, a model teacher. His definiteness of aim, his efforts to arouse interest, and to awaken the imagination, his ability to adapt himself to his pupils' needs, his high idea of learning for its own sake, all are admirable. Yet it was his personality, his sympathy for his pupils, his untiring efforts in their behalf, above all, the force of his own example, which were the most potent factors in giving him an ascendancy over their hearts and minds. The enthusiasm with which they studied under him, the veneration in which they held him, the loyalty with which they followed the narrow but safe path of tradition which he had marked out for them, leave no room for doubt as to his pre-eminence in his day as a scholar and teacher. His name, his methods, became a tradition; a hundred years afterwards, an ardent admirer gave

---

(1) "Habeas et singulis his ordinibus magistros suos, ne, vacantes otio, vagi discurrant per loca vel inanes exerceant ludos vel aliis mancipentur ineptiis," *Ep.* 114, p. 169. Cf. "Non per campos discurrentes" et seq., p. 168. (2) *Carmen*, 97, M. G. H. Poet. Lat. Med. Aev., I, pp. 321, 322.

(3) *Carmen*, 93, *ibid.*, pp. 319, 320.

(4) *In Dormiturio*, *Carmen*, 96, *ibid.*, p. 321.

him the palm over Priscian and Donatus.[1] Even before
the end of Charles' reign his influence is discernible.
Leidrad of Lyons had established his schools. The one,
the "scola cantorum," prepared many teachers of the chant,
while the 'other, the "scola lectorum," made considerable
progress in the study of the Scriptures.[2] Under Theodulph
of Orleans the liberal arts were being studied and many
beautiful as well as accurate manuscripts produced.[3] Arno
of Bavaria, too, maintained cathedral schools, founded a
library of one hundred and fifty books, and established a
chronicle. At Corbie, likewise, and at St. Riquier, where
Alcuin's pupils Adalhard and Angilbert lived, as well as at
Metz, Fleury, and St. Amands, there was a wonderful
revival.[4]

And so, unimportant as the educational works of Alcuin
appear, mediocre, ill-digested as his learning undoubtedly
was, yet by reason of his own untiring enthusiasm and the
splendid loyalty of his pupils, he was enabled to effect a
real renaissance in Frankland. Though he added nothing
to the world's knowledge, he assimilated the learning of his
predecessors in such measure that it was the more securely
transmitted to future ages.

(1) *Notatio Nothkeri*, Duemmler, *Formelbuch des Bischofs Sa-
lomo*, p. 72, quoted in Gaskoin, p. 245, note 3.
(2) Leidrad. *Ep.* 30, M. G. H. Epistol., IV., p. 543.
(3) M. G. H. Poet. Lat. Med. Aev., *op. cit.*, I, p. 544.
(4) Hauck, *op. cit.*, II, p. 196, and authorities there cited.

BIBLIOGRAPHY

I.—ORIGINAL SOURCES.

ALCUIN, *Opera Omnia*, 2 vols. Paris, 1851. (Migne, *Patrologia Latina*, C, CI). This is a reprint of the edition of Froben, published at Ratisbon, 1777.
    Carmina, ed. E. Duemmler (Monumenta Germaniae Historica; Poetarum Latinorum Medii Aevi, I, pp. 160-351).
    Epistolae, ed. E. Duemmler (M. G. H. Epistolarum, Vol. IV, pp. 1-481).
    Epistolae, ed. P. Jaffé ("Monumenta Alcuiniana" in Bibliotheca Rerum Germanicarum, Vol. VI, pp. 131-901, Berlin, 1867).
    Vita, ed. W. Arndt (M. G. H. SS. XV, pt. I, pp. 182-197. Also in Jaffé, *op. cit.*, Vol. VI, pp. 1-34).
    Vita Sancti Willibrordi, Jaffé, *op. cit.*, Vol. VI. pp. 35-79.
CAPITULARIA REGUM FRANCORUM, M. G. H. Legum, sect. II, Vols. I, II. Ed. A. Boretius et V. Krause. Berolini, 1883-1897.
EINHART, *Vita Caroli Magni imperatoris*, M. G. H. SS. II, pp. 443-463. *Annales*, in M. G. H. SS., Vol. I, pp. 124-218.
MONUMENTA CAROLINI (Bibliotheca Rerum Germanicarum, ed. Jaffé, Vol. IV).

II.—SECONDARY SOURCES.

BALL, W. R. R., *A Short Account of the History of Mathematics*, 3d ed., London, 1901.
BROCKMAN, F. J., *System der Chronologie*. Stuttgart, 1883.
BURSIAN, C., *Geschichte der Classischen Philologie in Deutschland*. Vol. I, München, 1883.
CAJORI, F., *A History of Elementary Mathematics*. New York, 1896.
CANTOR, M., *Mathematische Beiträge zum Kulturleben der Völker*. Halle, 1863.
CANTOR, M., *Die Römischen Agrimensoren und ihre Stellung in der Geschichte der Feldmesserkunst*. Leipzig, 1875.
CANTOR, M., *Vorlesungen über Geschichte der Mathematik*, Vol. I, II Auflage. Leipzig, 1894-1900.
COMPARETTI, D., *Virgil in the Middle Ages*. Translated by E. F. M. Benecke, London, 1895.
DENK, V. M., OTTO, *Geschichte des Gallo-Frankischen Unterrichts-und Bildungswesens von den Ältesten Zeiten bis auf Karl den Grossen*. Mainz, 1892.
DRANE, A. T., *Christian Schools and Scholars*. Second edition. London, 1881.
DUMMLER, E., *Alcuinus* in Neues Archiv der Gesellschaft für ältere Deutsche Geschichtskunde, Vol. IV, 1879, pp. 118-139

DUEMMLER, E., *Alchuinstudien* (Sitzungsberichte der k. Preussischen Akademie der Wissenschaften, 1891, pp. 495-523).

DUEMMLER, E., *Zur Lebensgeschichte Alchuins,* in Neues Archiv, Vol. 18, pp. 51-70.

EBERT, A., *Allgemeine Geschichte der Literatur des Mittelalters im Abendlande.* Leipzig, 1874-1887.

FRIEDLEIN, G., *Das Rechnen mit Columnen vor dem 10 Jahrhundert* (in Zeitschrift für Mathematik und Physik, Vol. IX).

FRIEDLEIN, G., *Die Zahlzeichen und das Elementare Rechnen der Griechen und Römer und des Christlichen Abendlandes vom 7 ten bis 13 ten Jahrhundert.* Erlangen, 1869.

GASKOIN, C. J. C., *Alcuin, his Life and his Work.* London, 1904.

HADDAN, A. W., *Remains.* Edited by A. P. Forbes. London, 1876.

HADDAN, A. W., and STUBBS, W., *Councils and Ecclesiastical Documents Relating to Great Britain and Ireland,* Vol. III. Oxford, 1869-1873.

HANKEL, H., *Zur Geschichte der Mathematik im Alterthum und Mittelalter.* Leipzig, 1874.

HATCH, E., *The Growth of Church Institutions.* London, 1895.

HAUCK, A., *Kirchengeschichte Deutschlands.* Zweiter Theil. Die Karolingerzeit. Zweite Auflage. Leipzig, 1900.

HAURÉAU, B., *De la philosophie scolastique,* 2 Vols. Paris, 1850.

HARNACK, A., *Histoy of Dogma,* Vol. V. Translated by Neil Buchanan. Boston, 1899.

HEFELE, C. J., *Conciliengeschichte.* Zweite Auflage. Freiburg, 1873.

Histoire Littéraire de la France, Vols. IV, V, VI.

KLEINCLAUSZ, *L'empire Carolingien ses origines et ses transformations.* (Hachette, Paris, 1902.)

LORENTZ, F., *Alcuin's Leben.* Halle, 1829.

MANITIUS, M., *Beiträge zur Geschichte Römischer Dichter im Mittelalter* (Philologus—Zeitschrift für das Classische Alterthum, Bde. 47, 48, 49, 50, 51, 52, 56).

MASIUS, H., *Die Erziehung im Mittelalter* (ap. K. A. Schmid, Geschichte der Erziehung, II, I. Stuttgart, 1892, pp. 94-333).

MOMBERT, *A History of Charles the Great.* London, 1888.

MONNIER, F., *Alcuin et son influence littéraire, religieuse, et politique chez les Francs.* Paris, 1853.

MONNIER, F., *Alcuin et Charlemagne.* Paris, 1864.

MORLEY, H., *English Writers,* Vol. II. London, 1888.

MULLANY, P. F. (Brother Azarias), *Educational Essays.* Chicago, 1896.

MULLINGER, J. B., *Schools of Charles the Great and the Restoration of Education in the Ninth Century.* London, 1877.

NAUMAN, EMIL, *The History of Music,* 2 vols.

NORDEN, E., *Die Antike Kunstprosa vom 6ten Jahrhundert vor Christus bis in die Zeit der Renaissance,* 2 vols. Leipzig, 1898.

PARKER, H., *The Seven Liberal Arts.* English Historical Review. Vol. V, July, 1890.

PRANTL, C., *Geschichte der Logik im Abendlande.* Bd. II. Zweite Auflage. Leipzig, 1885.

RASHDALL, H., *The Universities of Europe in the Middle Ages,* 3 vols. Oxford, 1895.

ROGER, M., *L'Enseignement des lettres classiques d'Ausone à Alcuin, Introduction à l'histoire des écoles carolingiennes,* Paris, 1905.

SCHMIDT, K. A., *Geschichte der Erzeihung vom Anfang an bis auf unsere Zeit, bearbeitet in Gemeinschaft mit einer Anzahl von Ge-*

lehrten und Schulmännern, 5 vols. Stuttgart, 1884-1902.

SICKEL, TH., *Alcuinstudien* I (Sitzungsberichte d. philosoph. Histor. Classe d. kais. Akademie der Wissenschaften), Vol. LXXIX (1875), pp. 461-550.

SPECHT, F. A., *Geschichte des Unterrichtswesens in Deutschland . . . bis zur Mitte des dreizehnten Jahrhunderts.* Stutttgart, 1883.

WATTENBACH, W., *Das Schriftwesen im Mittelalter.* 3 Auflage. Leipzig, 1896.

WERNER, K., *Alcuin und sein Jahrhundert.* Paderborn, 1876.

WERNER, K., *Beda der Ehrwurdige und seine Zeit.* Wien, 1881.

WEST, A. F., *Alcuin and the Rise of the Christian Schools* (Great Educators). London, 1893.

VITA

The author of this dissertation, Rolph Barlow Page, was born at Concord, Ontario, Canada, on December 11th., 1875. He graduated from the University of Toronto in 1897, with the degree of A. B., obtaining honors in Modern Languages and History. In 1901, he obtained his degree of A. M. from the same University. During the years 1902-04, he was Scholar and Fellow in European History at Columbia University, where he studied History and allied subjects under the Faculty of Political Science. From 1904 to 1909, he has been instructor in History and Civics at the High School of Commerce, New York City. In addition to the above dissertation, the author has written an essay, entitled *Life and Times of Chaucer*. This was published in the Report of the Ontario Educational Association for 1901.

CPSIA information can be obtained
at www.ICGtesting.com
Printed in the USA
BVHW031614051120
592525BV00005BA/250